Aspen

Bob D'Antonio

FALCON®

Guilford, Connecticut

An imprint of The Globe Pequot Press

This book is dedicated to my wife Laurel and to my three children Jeremy, Adam and Rachael. All of you make my life better.

AFALCONGUIDE ®

Copyright © 2001 by The Globe Pequot Press

Falcon and FalconGuide are registered trademarks of The Globe Pequot Press.

Cover photo: Index Stock Imagery

Library of Congress Cataloging-in-Publication Data
D'Antonio, Bob.
   Mountain biking Aspen / by Bob D'Antonio.—1st ed.
      p. cm.
   ISBN 1-56044-739-7
      1. All-terrain cycling—Colorado—Aspen—Guidebooks. 2. Aspen (Colo.)—Guidebooks.
1. Title.
GV1045.5.C62 A863 2001
796.6'3'0978843—dc21

                                                        2001023820

Manufactured in the United States of America
First Edition/First Printing

 Text pages printed on recycled paper.

Table of Contents

Mountain Biking Aspen Map Legend

Interstate		Campground	▲
U.S. Highway		Picnic Area	
State or Other Principal Road		Buildings	■
Forest Road	000	Peak/Elevation	4,507 ft.
Interstate Highway		Elevation	x 4,507 ft.
Paved Road		Gate	
Bike Path		Parking Area	P
Trail (doubletrack)		Overlook/Viewpoint	
Trail (singletrack)		Pass	
Trailhead		Ski Lift	
Trail Marker		Forest/Wilderness Boundary	
Waterway		Map Orientation	N
Lake/Reservoir			
Bog		Scale	0 0.5 1 MILES
City	or ○		

Aspen/Roaring Fork Valley Area

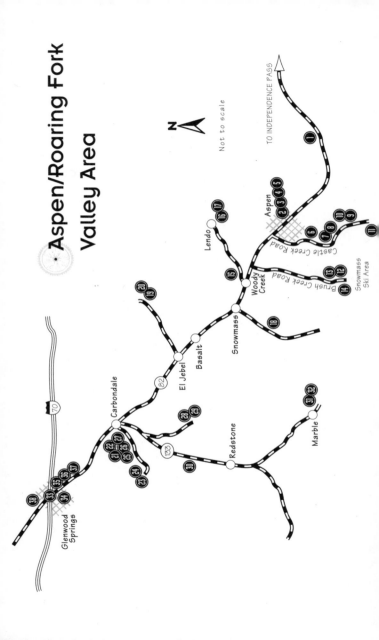

Not to scale

N

TO INDEPENDENCE PASS

Aspen

Castle Creek Road

Brush Creek Road

Snowmass Ski Area

Woody Creek

Lendo

Snowmass

Basalt

El Jebel

Carbondale

Glenwood Springs

Redstone

Marble

70

82

133

Get Ready to CRANK!

Where to ride? It's a quandary that faces every mountain biker, beginner or expert, local or tourist.

If you're new to the area, where do you start? If you're a long-time local, how do you avoid the rut of riding the same old trails week after week? And how do you find new terrain that's challenging but not overwhelming? Or an easier ride for when your not-so-serious buddies come along?

Welcome to *Mountain Biking Aspen*. Here are thirty-eight rides ranging from easy doubletrack routes to smooth singletrack to bravado-busting boulder fields. The rides are described in plain language, with accurate distances and ratings for physical and technical difficulty. Each entry offers a wealth of detailed information that's easy to read and use, from an armchair or on the trail.

My aim is threefold: to help you choose a ride that's appropriate for your fitness and skill level; to make it easy to find the trailhead; and to help you complete the ride safely, without getting lost. Take care of those basics and fun is bound to break loose.

Aspen

What to Expect

The rides in the Aspen and Roaring Fork Valley area cover a wide variety of terrain—from high-desert flats and mountains to forested mountain ridges. The trails can be steep and rough, and the weather—well, things change quickly in the Roaring Fork Valley. In the summertime there is little relief from the ever-present sun. At higher elevations, thunderstorms are common in summer, and snowfall can occur in any month of the year. Be prepared for all possible conditions.

Rugged terrain requires preparedness. Get in good shape before you attempt these rides, and know your limits. Clean and maintain your bike frequently. Before each ride check tires, rims, brakes, handlebars, seat, shifters, derailleurs, and chain to make sure they survived the last ride and are functioning properly.

A **helmet** is essential for safe mountain biking; it can prevent serious injuries if not save your life. Cycling **gloves** are another essential piece of safety equipment that can save hands from cuts and bruises from falls, encroaching branches, and rocks. They also improve your grip and comfort on the handlebars.

Always pack at least one (filled) water bottle—preferably two—or the equivalent. Rides in Aspen and Roaring Fork Valley start at high **altitude** and you'll want **more water** than you typically carry at lower elevations. A gallon is not too much on long mountain rides. A snack such as fruit or sports energy bars can keep those mighty thighs cranking for hours and prevent dreaded "bonk"—the sudden loss of energy when your body runs out of fuel.

Dress for the weather and pack a wind- and waterproof jacket just in case, especially in the spring and fall. The Colorado high-country summer sun packs a wallop. Don't forget sunglasses, sunscreen, and lip balm. Insects can be a problem for a short period in the summer; in wet years you may want to carry insect repellent.

It's wise to carry a small **tool kit** with appropriate tools for your bike, a spare tube, and a patch kit. A **tire pump** is a must. You'll want to fill your tubes with leak-repair goo; the desert is full of thorns and spines. Consider thicker, thorn-resistant tubes.

This book is designed to be easily carried in a pocket or bike bag, and the maps and ride descriptions will help anyone unfamiliar with the trails. U.S. Geological Survey (USGS) topographic maps can provide a more detailed view of the terrain, but ride routes may not be shown. The correct topo maps are listed for each ride. Finally—I'll say it again—**always wear a helmet.**

The **weather** on the western slope of Colorado's mountains and high desert spans the range of North American extremes. On the highest rides in the Aspen and Roaring Fork Valley area, snow is common from early November through early May. Summer highs routinely top eighty degrees F in the higher desert country. In general, higher elevations are cooler (by as much as six degrees F for every 1,000 feet) and windier. If you drive to the trailhead for the rides at higher elevation, play it safe and take a variety of clothes in the car to match the weather you're likely to encounter.

That said, we ride here almost year-round. Most of the trails around Aspen and the Roaring Fork Valley are best between May and October. The higher-elevation trails are best from June through October, although in dry years they can be ridden well into November. The best **seasons** to ride are summer and fall. Bear in mind that hunting seasons may overlap the good fall riding weather. Check with the Colorado Division of Wildlife for current hunting seasons. (See the appendix.) If you choose to ride where hunts are taking place, a blaze orange vest is a sensible precaution.

Afternoon **thunderstorms** are common during July, August, and September. These storms often appear suddenly and can be severe, with hail, snow, high wind, and lightning. If caught in a thunderstorm, get off high ridges and take shelter in a low-lying area or in a vehicle. Do not remain under lone trees. In the higher mountains during thunderstorm season, the mornings generally dawn sweet and clear, the air refreshed by yesterday's showers. Up here, it's a good idea to complete your day's riding by noon.

The rides in this book vary from 5,000 feet to more than 12,000 feet in elevation, which means you really can ride dirt most of the year, somewhere.

Please stay off wet, muddy trails—the soil damage and erosion one rider can cause is simply too great. Most of the high-mountain rides do not dry out until well into June or early July, so take this into consideration when planning your trip into the high country.

The name of the game in Aspen and the Roaring Fork Valley is **awesome, high-mountain riding.** Some of the best singletrack riding and scenery in the state of Colorado can found in the beautiful high country of Aspen and the Roaring Fork Valley. Respect other trail users and stay **on the trail.**

Rules of the Trail

If every mountain biker always yielded the right-of-way, stayed on the trail, avoided wet or muddy trails, never cut switchbacks, always rode in control, showed respect for other trail users, and carried out every last scrap of what was carried in (candy wrappers and bike-part debris included)—in short, if we all *did the right thing*—we wouldn't need a list of rules governing our behavior.

Fact is, most mountain bikers are conscientious and are trying to do the right thing. No one becomes good at something as demanding and painful as grunting up mountainsides by cheating. Most of us don't need rules. But we do need knowledge of what exactly is the right thing to do.

Here are some guidelines, reprinted with permission from the International Mountain Bicycling Association. The basic idea is to prevent or minimize damage to land, water, plants, and wildlife, and to avoid conflicts with other backcountry visitors and trail users. Ride with respect.

IMBA Rules of the Trail

Thousands of miles of dirt trails have been closed to mountain bicyclists. The irresponsible riding habits of a few riders have been a factor. Do your part to maintain trail access by observing the following rules of the trail, formulated by the International Mountain Bicycling Association (IMBA). IMBA's mission is to promote environmentally sound and socially responsible mountain biking.

1. Ride on open trails only. Respect trail and road closures (ask if not sure), avoid possible trespass on private land, and obtain permits and authorization as may be required. Federal wilderness areas are closed to bicycles and all other mechanized and motorized equipment. The way you ride will influence trail management decisions and policies.

2. Leave no trace. Be sensitive to the dirt beneath you. Even on open (legal) trails, you should not ride under conditions where you will leave evidence of your passing, such as on certain soils after a rain. Recognize different types of soils and trail construction; practice low-impact cycling. This also means staying on existing trails and not creating new ones. Be sure to pack out at least as much as you pack in. Some of the rides feature optional side hikes into wilderness areas. Be a low-impact hiker, also.

3. Control your bicycle! Inattention for even a second can cause problems. Obey all bicycle speed regulations and recommendations.

4. Always yield trail. Make known your approach well in advance. A friendly greeting (or bell) is considerate and works well; don't startle others. Show your respect when passing by, slowing to a walking pace or even stopping. Anticipate other trail users at corners and blind spots.

5. Never spook animals. All animals are startled by an unannounced approach, a sudden movement, or a loud noise. This can be dangerous for you, others, and the animals. Give animals extra room and time to adjust to you. When passing horses use special care and follow directions from the horseback riders (dismount and ask if uncertain). Chasing cattle and disturbing wildlife is a serious offense. Leave gates as you found them, or as marked.

6. Plan ahead. Know your equipment, your ability, and the area in which you are riding—and prepare accordingly. Be self-sufficient at all times, keep your equipment in good repair, and carry necessary supplies for changes in weather or other conditions. A well-executed trip is a satisfaction to you and not a burden or offense to others. Always wear a helmet.

Keep trails open by setting a good example of environmentally sound and socially responsible off-road cycling.

How to Use This Guide

Mountain Biking Aspen describes thirty-eight mountain bike rides in their entirety. Many of the featured rides are loops, beginning and ending at the same point but coming and going on different trails. Loops are by far the most popular type of ride, and we're lucky to have so many in the area.

Be forewarned, however: The difficulty of a loop may change dramatically depending on which direction you ride around the loop. If you are unfamiliar with the rides in this book, try them first as described here. The directions follow the path of least resistance and most fun (which does not necessarily mean easy). After you've been over the terrain, you can determine whether a given loop would be fun—or even feasible—in the reverse direction. Some trails are designated as one-way, so you don't have a choice.

Portions of some rides follow maintained dirt or even paved roads. A word about mountain dirt roads: Because the weather is so unstable and wet during the winter months, many dirt roads, though officially maintained, don't actually receive much attention. The surface may become loose because of accumulating sand and gravel, and washboarded roads can be a pain.

Each ride description follows the same format:

Number: Rides are cross-referenced by number throughout this book. In many cases, parts of rides or entire routes can be linked to other rides for longer rides or variations on a standard route. These opportunities are noted, followed by "see Ride(s) #."

Name: For the most part, I have relied on official names of trails, roads, and natural features as shown on U.S. Geological Survey maps. In some cases deference was given to long-term local custom.

Location: Directions and approximate distances are from Aspen, Snowmass, Carbondale, or Glenwood Springs.

Distance: The length of the ride in miles, given as a loop, one-way (if shuttled), or out and back.

Time: A conservative estimate of how long it takes to complete the ride: for example, 1 to 2 hours. *The time listed is the actual riding time and does not include rest stops.* Strong, skilled riders may be able to do a given ride in less than the estimated time, while other riders may take considerably longer. Also bear in mind that severe weather, changes in trail conditions, or mechanical problems may prolong a ride.

Tread: The type of road or trail: paved road, maintained dirt road, doubletrack road, or singletrack.

Aerobic level: The level of physical effort required to complete the ride: easy, moderate, or strenuous.
    Easy: Flat or gently rolling terrain, with no steep or prolonged climbs.
    Moderate: Some hills; the climbs may be short and fairly steep, or long and gradual. There may be short hills that less-fit riders will want to walk.

8

Strenuous: Frequent or prolonged climbs steep enough to require riding in the lowest gear; requires a high level of aerobic fitness, power, and endurance (typically acquired through many hours of riding and proper training). Less-fit riders may need to walk.

Many rides are mostly easy and moderate but may have short strenuous sections. Other rides are mostly strenuous and should be attempted only after a complete medical checkup and implant of a second heart, preferably a *big* one. Also be aware that flailing through a highly technical section can be exhausting, even on the flats. Good riding skills and a relaxed stance on the bike save energy.

Finally, any ride can be strenuous if you ride it hard and fast. Conversely, the pain of a lung-burning climb becomes easier to tolerate as your fitness level improves. Learn to pace yourself and remember to schedule easy rides and rest days into your calendar.

Technical difficulty: The level of bike handling skills needed to complete the ride upright and in one piece. Technical difficulty is rated on a scale of 1 to 5, with 1 being the easiest and 5 the hardest.

Level 1: Smooth tread; road or doubletrack; no obstacles, ruts, or steeps. Requires basic bike-handling skills.

Level 2: Mostly smooth tread; wide, well-groomed singletrack or road/doubletrack with minor ruts, loose gravel, or sand.

Level 3: Irregular tread with some rough sections; slickrock, singletrack, or doubletrack with obvious route choices; some steep sections; occasional obstacles may include small rocks, roots, water bars, ruts, loose gravel or sand, and sharp turns or broad, open switchbacks.

Level 4: Rough tread with few smooth places; singletrack or rough doubletrack with limited route choices; steep sections, some with obstacles; obstacles are numerous and varied, including rocks, roots, branches, ruts, sidehills, narrow tread, loose gravel or sand, and switchbacks. Most slickrock falls in this level.

Level 5: Continuously broken, rocky, root-infested, or trenched tread; singletrack or extremely rough doubletrack with few route choices; frequent, sudden, and severe changes in gradient; some slopes so steep that wheels lift off the ground; obstacles are nearly continuous and may include boulders, logs, water, large holes, deep ruts, ledges, piles of loose gravel, steep sidehills, encroaching trees, and tight switchbacks.

I've also added plus (+) and minus (-) symbols to cover gray areas between given levels of difficulty: a 4+ obstacle is harder than a 4, but easier than a 5-. A stretch of trail rated 5+ would be unrideable by all but the most skilled riders.

Again, most of the rides in this book cover varied terrain, with an ever-changing degree of technical difficulty. Some trails run smooth with only occasional obstacles, and other trails are seemingly nothing but obstacles. The path of least resistance, or *line*, is where you find it. In general, most obstacles are more challenging if you encounter them while climbing rather than while descending. On the other hand, in heavy surf (e.g., boulder fields, tangles of downfall, cliffs), fear plays a larger role when facing downhill.

Understand that different riders have different strengths and weaknesses. Some folks can scramble over logs and boulders without a grunt, but they crash head over heels on every switchback turn. Some fly down the steepest slopes and others freeze. Some riders climb like the wind and others just blow . . . and walk.

10

The key to overcoming "technical difficulties" is practice: keep trying. Follow a rider who makes it look easy, and don't hesitate to ask for constructive criticism. Try shifting your weight (good riders move a lot, front to back, side to side, and up and down) and experimenting with balance and momentum. Find a smooth patch of lawn and practice riding as slowly as possible, even balancing in a "track stand" (described in the glossary). This will give you more confidence—and more time to recover or bail out— the next time the trail rears up and bites.

Hazards: A list of dangers that may be encountered on a ride, including traffic, weather, trail obstacles and conditions, risky stream crossings, obscure trails, and other perils. Remember: conditions may change at any time. Be prepared for storms, new fences, deadfall, missing trail signs, and mechanical failure. Fatigue, heat, cold, and/or dehydration may impair judgment. Always wear a helmet and other safety equipment. Ride in control at all times. If a section of trail seems too difficult for you, it's cooler to get off and walk your bike through the bad section than fly over your handlebars and break your collarbone.

Highlights: Special features or qualities that make a ride worth doing (as if we needed an excuse!): scenery, fun singletrack, challenging climbs, or chances to see wildlife.

Land status: A list of managing agencies or landowners. Most of the rides in this book are on public land belonging to one of the cities, White River National Forest, or the Bureau of Land Management. These agencies along with the help of many volunteers have done a great job in creating a wonderful mountain bike area.

Maps: A list of available maps. The USGS of Pitkin, Gunnison, and Garfield Counties were used for most rides. The Colorado Atlas published by DeLorme, mapping at a scale of 1:250,000, gives a good topographic overview. USGS topographic maps in the 7.5-minute series give a close-up look at terrain. Not all routes are shown on official maps.

Access: How to find the trailhead or the start of the ride, starting from a major street or highway in or around Aspen and the Roaring Fork Valley. If you're lucky enough to live near one of the rides, you may be able to pedal to the start. For most riders, it'll be necessary to drive to the trailhead, or desirable to do a shuttle with two cars.

The ride: A mile-by-mile list of key points—landmarks, notable climbs and descents, wash/stream crossings, obstacles, hazards, major turns and junctions—along the ride. All distances were measured to the nearest tenth of a mile with a carefully calibrated cyclometer. As a result, you will find a cyclometer to be very useful for following the descriptions. Terrain, riding technique, and even tire pressure can affect odometer readings, so treat all mileages as approximates. Trails were precisely mapped using the USGS 7.5-minute topographic maps as a reference. A GPS (Global Positioning System) receiver was used to supplement more traditional methods of land navigation where landmarks were obscure.

One last reminder: the real world is changing all the time. The information presented here is as accurate and up-to-date as possible, but there are no guarantees out in the backcountry. You alone are responsible for your safety and for the choices you make on the trail. However, it's generally a good idea to bike with a partner—or to let somebody know where you're going and when you expect to return from an especially long or challenging ride.

The Name Game

Mountain bikers often assign their own descriptive nick-names to trails. These nicknames may help to distinguish or describe certain parts of the overall ride, but only for the group of people that knows the nickname. All too often the nicknames are meaningless—or misleading—to cyclists who haven't spun their pedals on the weekly group ride.

For the sake of clarity, I stuck to the official (or at least most widely accepted) names for the trails and roads described in this book. When a route is commonly known by more than one name, the other names are mentioned. If you know them by some other name, or if you come up with nicknames that peg the personalities of these rides, then by all means share them with your riding buddies.

Help Us Keep This Guide Up to Date

Every effort has been made by the author and editors to make this guide as accurate and useful as possible. However, many things can change after a guide is published—trails are rerouted, regulations change, techniques evolve, facilities come under new management, etc.

We would love to hear from you concerning your experiences with this guide and how you feel it could be improved and be kept up to date. While we may not be able to respond to all comments and suggestions, we'll take them to heart and we'll also make certain to share them with the author. Please send your comments and suggestions to the following address:

The Globe Pequot Press
Reader Response/Editorial Department
P.O. Box 480
Guilford, CT 06437

Or you may e-mail us at:

editorial@globe-pequot.com

Thanks for your input, and happy travels!

Lincoln Creek Road

Location: 10 miles east of downtown Aspen.

Distance: 12.2 miles out and back.

Time: 1.5 to 2.5 hours.

Tread: 12.2 miles on doubletrack.

Aerobic level: Moderate with a few short, steep climbs.

Technical difficulty: 1 to 2.

Hazards: Car and four-wheeler traffic. This road is very crowded during weekends in the summer months.

Highlights: Nice beginner's ride along Lincoln Creek to Grizzly Reservoir; great views of Truro, Larson, and Grizzly Peaks; opportunities to soak in the river.

Land status: White River National Forest.

Maps: USGS, Pitkin County.

Access: From downtown Aspen, ride or drive your car ten miles up Independence Pass (Colorado 82) to Lincoln Creek Road and a parking area on the right.

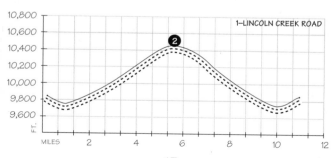

·Lincoln Creek Road

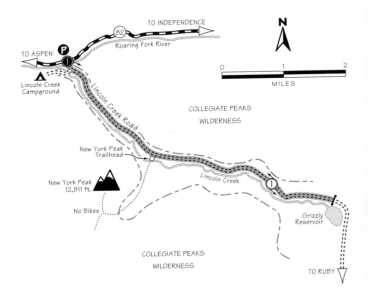

The ride

0.0 From the parking area take Lincoln Creek Road down along the Roaring Fork River.

0.5 Entrance to Lincoln Creek Campground goes right; continue on the main road past several national forest campsites.

1.2 Climb up a short, steep hill.

1.6 Another short, steep hill.

2.0 Lincoln Creek on right. Great spot to soak in the "tubs."

3.2 New York Peak Trailhead on the right. The trail is off-limits to cyclists. Continue straight.

3.5 The road opens up into a beautiful meadow with spectacular views.

4.0 Cross over a viaduct.

6.1 Arrive at Grizzly Reservoir. Take a break and enjoy the views before heading back to the parking area.

12.2 Back at the parking area.

Smuggler Mountain

Location: 1 mile northeast of downtown Aspen.

Distance: 3.0 miles out and back.

Time: 0.5 to 1 hour.

Tread: 3.0 miles on doubletrack.

Aerobic level: Moderate with a long climb up Smuggler Mountain.

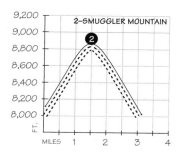

· Smuggler Mountain

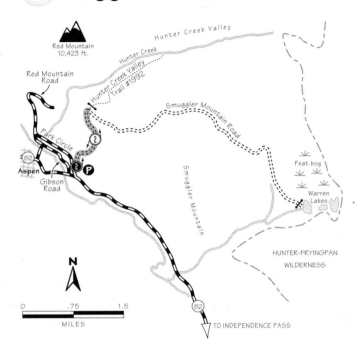

Technical difficulty: 2.

Hazards: This is a very popular hiking, running, and biking trail. Show respect to other trail users and keep your speed in check on the downhill sections.

Highlights: A popular road in summer months, with easy access to several backcountry trails.

Land status: White River National Forest.

Maps: USGS, Pitkin County.

Access: The mileage starts at the junction of Gibson Road and Smuggler Mountain Road.

The ride

0.0   Pedal up Smuggler Mountain Road past the Smuggler Mine. This road is very popular with other trail users. Be courteous.

0.8   Excellent views down the Roaring Fork Valley and out to Snowmass, Capitol, and Pyramid Peaks.

1.1   Grade increases as you crank up to a three-way trail junction.

1.5   Arrive at a road junction. Going straight takes you to Warren Lakes; going left drops you down into the Hunter Creek Valley. Turn around and cruise back into Aspen.

3.0   Back at Gibson Road.

Hunter Creek

Location: 1 mile northeast of downtown Aspen.

Distance: 7.6-mile loop.

Time: 1.5 to 2.5 hours.

Tread: 2.6 miles on singletrack; 3.0 miles on doubletrack; 2 miles on paved roads.

Aerobic level: Moderate with a long climb up Smuggler Mountain.

Technical difficulty: 3+ on the singletrack; 3 on double-track.

Hazards: This is a very popular hiking, running, and biking trail. Show respect to other trail users and keep your speed in check on the downhill sections.

Highlights: A great ride with a lot of variety and access to miles of biking trails. There is a great singletrack section and a fun, fast downhill back to town.

Land status: White River National Forest.

Maps: USGS, Pitkin County.

Access: The mileage starts at the junction of Gibson Road and Smuggler Mountain Road.

The ride

0.0 Pedal up Smuggler Mountain Road past the Smuggler Mine. This road is very popular with other trail users. Be courteous.

0.8 Excellent views down the Roaring Fork Valley.

1.1 Grade increases as you crank up to a three-way trail junction.

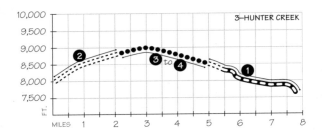

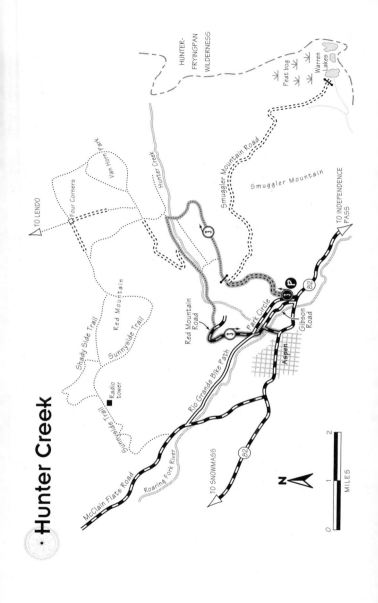

Hunter Creek

HUNTER-
FRYINGPAN
WILDERNESS

Warren
Lakes

Peat bog

Smuggler Mountain Road

Smuggler Mountain

TO INDEPENDENCE
PASS

82

Hunter Creek

Four Corners

Van Horn Park

TO LENDO

Shady Side Trail

Red Mountain

Sunnyside Trail

Red Mountain Road

Park Circle

Gibson Road

Aspen

82

Rio Grande Bike Path

Sunnyside Trail

Radio
Tower

McClain Flats Road

Roaring Fork River

TO SNOWMASS

82

N

0   1   2
MILES

1.5	Go left on a doubletrack road through the open gate.
2.0	Drop down steep, rocky tread to an old mine site on the right.
2.3	Go right at the mine, now on a tight, rocky singletrack trail. Follow this wonderful and sometimes difficult (4) trail down to the Hunter Creek Trail.
3.4	Go right on the Hunter Creek Trail, crossing over the bridge. Make a quick left down the beautiful trail along Hunter Creek.
4.2	Go left at trail junction.
4.3	Go right down sweet, rocky singletrack to a trail junction.
4.8	Continue straight down very rocky tread to Benedict Bridge. Cross over the bridge to a paved road.
5.3	Go right on paved road to a trail on the left.
5.4	Go down the tight singletrack to Red Mountain Road. Fly down the steep paved road (watch out for car traffic).
7.6	Arrive at Main Street and the Hotel Jerome Bar.

Warren Lakes

Location: 1 mile northeast of downtown Aspen.

Distance: 11.2 miles.

Time: 2 to 3 hours.

Tread: 11.2 mile on rough, rocky doubletrack.

Aerobic level: Strenuous uphill climb for more than 4 miles.

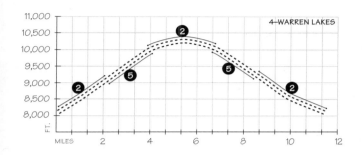

Technical difficulty: 5 on the rocky uphill climb past the microwave tower.

Hazards: Very rocky tread and four-wheel traffic. The uphill climb past the tower is unrelenting and the ride will test the skills and aerobic capacity of the best cyclists.

Highlights: Great views and a long uphill to Warren Lakes (sadly, the lakes are gone).

Land status: White River National Forest.

Maps: USGS, Pitkin County.

Access: The mileage starts at the junction of Gibson Road and Smuggler Mountain Road.

The ride

0.0 Begin a long climb up past the Smuggler Mine, past several homes to a three-way trail junction.

1.5 Continue straight up a steep (3+) doubletrack road to a flat area.

1.9 Arrive at a large platform area in a nice meadow. Go right up a steep section. Things start to get serious from this point on. If you are feeling weak you might

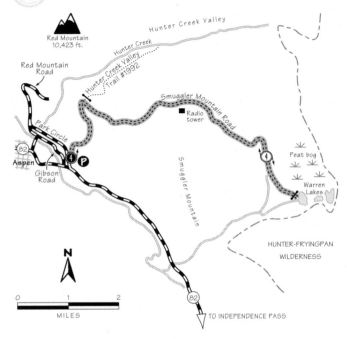

·Warren Lakes

Red Mountain
10,423 ft.

Red Mountain
Road

Hunter Creek Valley

Hunter Creek

Hunter Creek Valley
Trail #1992

Park Circle

Smuggler Mountain Road

Radio
tower

82

Aspen

Gibson
Road

Smuggler Mountain

4

Peat bog

Warren
Lakes

HUNTER-FRYINGPAN
WILDERNESS

N

0   1   2

MILES

82

TO INDEPENDENCE PASS

want to turn around here. Begin a mile of extremely steep, loose, rocky climbing.

2.6 Pass the microwave tower on the right. Continue up the steep, rocky hill.

3.0 Level tread for the moment. Enjoy—it doesn't last. Continue up steep switchbacks.

4.0 Climb up a short, steep hill.

4.2 Level tread: how nice!

4.6 Cross over a small stream in an open meadow. Continue straight up to Warren Lakes.

5.6 Arrive at Warren Lakes and take a well-deserved rest. Retrace your route back to start.

11.2 Back at the start.

Sunnyside Trail

Location: 1 mile northeast of downtown Aspen.

Distance: 15.8-mile loop.

Time: 2.5 to 3.5 hours.

Tread: 6.8 miles on singletrack; 7 miles on doubletrack; 2 miles on paved roads.

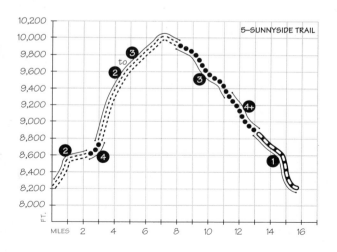

· Sunnyside Trail

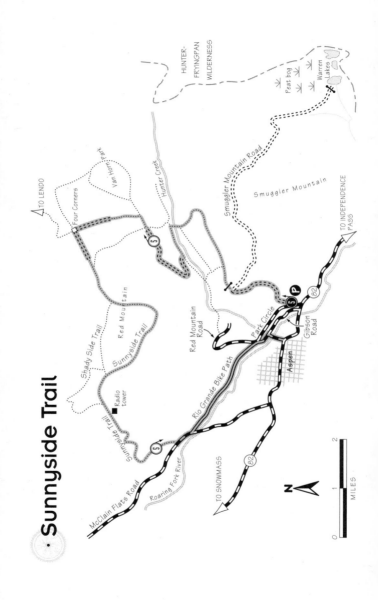

HUNTER-FRYINGPAN WILDERNESS

Peat bog

Warren Lakes

△ TO LENDO

Van Horn Park

Four Corners

Hunter Creek

Smuggler Mountain Road

Smuggler Mountain

Shady Side Trail

Red Mountain

Sunnyside Trail

Red Mountain Road

Park Circle

P

Radio tower

Sunnyside Trail

Aspen

Gibson Road

82

TO INDEPENDENCE PASS

Rio Grande Bike Path

Roaring Fork River

McClain Flats Road

82

TO SNOWMASS

N

0   1   2
MILES

Aerobic level: Strenuous with a long climb up Smuggler Mountain and up to Four Corners.

Technical difficulty: 4+ on the singletrack; 3 on double-track.

Hazards: This is a very popular hiking, running, and biking trail. Show respect to other trail users and keep your speed in check on the downhill sections. This is a demanding ride. Bring a lot of water and some energy bars.

Highlights: One of the best rides in the Aspen area, with lots of variety, several technical sections, loads of uphill climbing, and amazing singletrack through a spectacular aspen forest. Do this ride!

Land status: White River National Forest.

Maps: USGS, Pitkin County.

Access: The mileage starts at the junction of Gibson Road and Smuggler Mountain Road.

The ride

0.0 Pedal up Smuggler Mountain Road past the Smuggler Mine.

0.8 Excellent views down the Roaring Fork Valley.

1.1 Grade increases as you crank up to three-way trail junction.

1.5 Go left on a doubletrack road.

2.0 Drop down steep, rocky tread to an old mine site on the right.

2.3 Go right at the mine onto a tight, rocky singletrack trail. Follow this wonderful and sometimes difficult (4) trail down to the Hunter Creek Trail.

3.4 Go right on the Hunter Creek Trail, crossing over a bridge. Make a quick left down the beautiful trail along Hunter Creek to a trail junction.

4.4	Continue straight at the trail junction.
4.5	Go right and begin climbing up a smooth, four-wheel-drive road.
4.9	Enjoy the views out to the Maroon Bells.
5.4	Arrive at junction with Sunnyside Trail. Continue straight.
5.7	The Hunter Creek Trail goes right; continue straight to the Four Corners Trail junction.
6.7	Arrive at Four Corners. Go left on the Sunnyside Trail.
7.3	The Sunnyside Trail goes left; continue straight.
7.9	The trail forks. Go left down the often-wet double-track.
8.0	Bear left.
8.1	Trail turns to singletrack.
8.2	Climb up a short, steep hill. Follow the awesome, tight singletrack trail through a beautiful aspen forest. This is just incredible riding.
10.2	Shadyside Trail goes right. Continue straight.
10.8	Trail junction. Continue straight.
11.2	Microwave tower on left. Get ready for a steep, rocky (4) descent to McClain Flats Road.
12.1	Pass through a gate to a private drive. Cross over drive to a singletrack trail going down. Continue down on tight tread to road.
13.2	Go left down McClain Flats Road.
13.6	Go left onto the Rio Grande Trail and follow up to Red Mountain Road.
15.5	Go right on Red Mountain Road to Main Street.
15.8	Arrive at Main Street and Hotel Jerome Bar.

Midnight Mine Road

Location: 4 miles west of downtown Aspen.

Distance: 10.2 miles out and back.

Time: 1.5 to 2.5 hours.

Tread: Rough doubletrack.

Aerobic level: Moderate to strenuous.

Technical difficulty: 3 on the steep sections.

Hazards: Four-wheel-drive traffic and a fast downhill back to the start.

Highlights: Great uphill workout. Another way to reach Richmond Hill and the sun deck.

Land status: White River National Forest and private.

Maps: USGS, Pitkin County.

Access: From Main Street in Aspen travel west by bike or car on Colorado 82 to Maroon Creek Road. Go left on Ma-

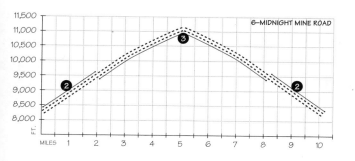

· Midnight Mine Road

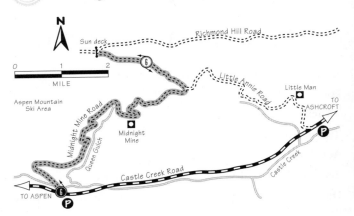

roon Creek Road for a short distance, make a quick left onto Castle Creek Road, and travel 3 miles to Midnight Mine Road and a small parking area.

The ride

0.0 Drop down Midnight Mine Road and cross over a bridge. The road climbs up past several homes.

0.7 The road climbs through a beautiful aspen forest.

1.4 Crank up steep switchbacks.

2.3 Climb past the Midnight Mine.

2.7 Keep those legs cranking. The tread becomes steep.

3.1 One last steep section before reaching Little Annie Road.

4.1 Junction with Little Annie Road. Go left up to the sun deck.

5.1 Arrive at the sun deck. Take a break before retracing your route back to Castle Creek Road.

10.2 Back at Midnight Mine Road.

Little Annie Road

Location: 8 miles west of downtown Aspen.

Distance: 8.2 miles out and back.

Time: 2 to 3 hours.

Tread: Doubletrack.

Aerobic level: Moderate with a long, gradual climb up Little Annie Road.

Technical difficulty: 2 to 3.

Hazards: Four-wheel-drive traffic.

Highlights: A great ride to the Aspen Mountain sun deck, and the most convenient and least strenuous way to reach

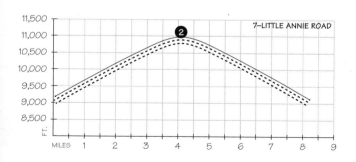

· Little Annie Road

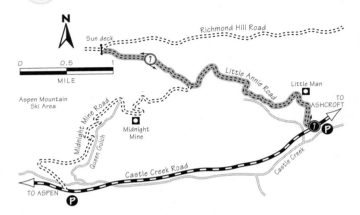

the Richmond Ridge or the top of Aspen Mountain. Expect spectacular views up Castle Valley and the surrounding high peaks.

Land status: White River National Forest.

Maps: USGS, Pitkin County.

Access: From Main Street in Aspen, travel west by bike or car on Colorado 82 to Maroon Creek Road. Go left on Maroon Creek Road for a short distance, make a quick left onto Castle Creek Road, and travel 7 miles to Little Annie Road and a small parking area on the right.

The ride

0.0 From the small parking area, cross Castle Creek Road and begin climbing up Little Annie Road.

0.7 Watch out for the little man on the right.

0.8	Dome home on the right.
1.1	The grade eases for the moment.
1.4	Go left at the road junction, and begin a steep climb.
1.8	Grade eases. Enjoy the spectacular views.
2.1	Continue straight past a private road.
2.3	Pass a log house.
2.6	The road bends to the right; amazing views up Castle Valley.
3.1	Junction with Midnight Mine Road. Continue straight up to the sun deck.
4.1	Arrive at the sun deck. Take a break, then retrace your route back to the parking area.
8.2	Back at Castle Creek Road.

Richmond Hill

Location: 8 miles west of downtown Aspen.

Distance: 23.4-mile loop.

Time: 3 to 5 hours.

Tread: 3.9 miles on paved road, 0.7 mile on singletrack, and 18.8 miles on dirt roads and doubletrack.

Aerobic level: Strenuous with several long, gradual, high-altitude climbs.

Technical difficulty: 2 to 4 on doubletrack. The downhill singletrack off Richmond Hill rates a solid 4.

Hazards: Four-wheel-drive traffic. This is a long ride at high altitude. Expect sudden weather changes; bring extra

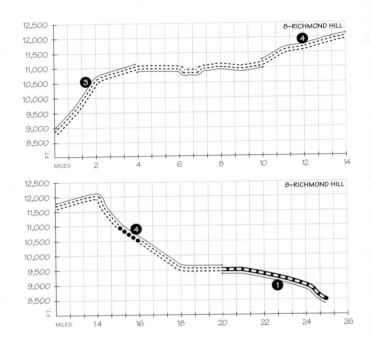

clothing, water, and food; and be prepared to be out on the trail for at least four hours. This ride should only be attempted by strong cyclists in excellent physical condition with the stamina to complete a high-altitude mountain bike tour.

Highlights: One of the best alpine rides in the Roaring Fork Valley; a great outing up to the top of Aspen Mountain, with a long ridge traverse along Richmond Ridge with some technical tread, and spectacular views of the surrounding high peaks and the Castle Valley.

Land status: White River National Forest.

Maps: USGS, Pitkin County.

Access: From Main Street in Aspen travel west by bike or car on Colorado 82 to Maroon Creek Road. Go left on Maroon Creek Road for a short distance, make a quick left onto Castle Creek Road, and travel 7 miles to Little Annie Road and a small parking area on the right.

The ride

0.0 From the small parking area, cross Castle Creek Road and begin climbing up Little Annie Road.

0.7 Watch out for the little man on the right.

0.8 Dome home on the right.

1.1 The grade eases for the moment.

1.4 Go left at a road junction and begin a steep climb.

1.8 Grade eases. Enjoy the spectacular views.

2.1 Continue straight past a private road.

2.3 Pass a log house.

2.6 The road bends to the right and you are hit with amazing views up Castle Valley.

• Richmond Hill

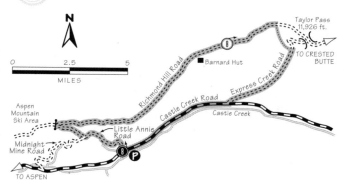

3.1	Junction with Midnight Mine Road. Continue straight up to the sun deck.
4.1	Arrive at the sun deck. After taking a break, go right on Richmond Hill Road.
4.9	Crank up a steep, loose, rocky hill (4).
5.2	Pass a hut on the right.
5.6	Road junction. Continue straight.
6.2	Make a nice downhill run.
6.9	Climb up a short, steep hill, then cruise on nice smooth tread.
8.4	Sign for the Collegiate Peaks Wilderness. Pedal through a wide-open meadow with beautiful wildflowers and sweeping views to the west and east.
8.9	Caution! Drop down a steep hill on loose, rocky tread (4).
9.9	Here comes a leg burner. Crank up a steep hill on loose tread (4).
10.7	Short steep hill. Having fun yet?
11.1	Road leads to the Barnard Hut. You continue straight, cruising on good tread to a large meadow.
12.1	Small stream crossing. Take a break here and enjoy this beautiful alpine meadow. Crank, push, or be pulled up a short, steep, nasty hill (5-).
12.4	Drop down a short, steep hill. Yes, you have to climb that monster hill looming ahead.
13.1	Begin a long, arduous climb up what seems to be a never-ending hill (4+).
13.9	Finally you've reached the top! Drop down a very steep (3+) hill to a trail junction.
15.1	Go right down the Express Creek (4) Connector Trail. Watch out for steep, loose, rocky sections.
15.9	Go right down Express Creek Road. Get ready for a long, wild, 4-mile downhill run. Keep your speed in check and watch out for loose, rocky sections.

19.5   Cross over a bridge and crank up to Castle Creek Road. Go right on Castle Creek Road and pedal down to Little Annie Road and your car.

23.4   Arrive back at your car.

Taylor Pass

Location: 11 miles south of downtown Aspen.

Distance: 11 miles out and back.

Time: 2 to 3.5 hours.

Tread: Rough, four-wheel road.

Aerobic level: Strenuous with a long climb to the top of Taylor Pass.

Technical difficulty: 2 to 3+.

Hazards: Watch out for four-wheel traffic and motorcycle riders. This is a popular road during the summer months. The ride back down the pass is extremely fast and rocky;

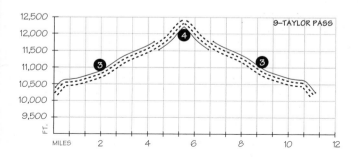

keep your speed in check and watch out for uphill traffic. Be prepared for sudden, violent weather changes and always expect snow on top of the pass. You should train at altitude before attempting this high-alpine ride.

Highlights: A great climb to the top of 11,928-foot Taylor Pass, with spectacular views out to the Collegiate Peaks Range, alpine flowers during the summer, and spectacular colors in early fall.

Land status: White River National Forest.

Maps: USGS, Pitkin County.

Access: From Main Street in Aspen, travel west by bike or car on Colorado 82 to Maroon Creek Road. Go left on Maroon Creek Road for a short distance, make a quick left onto Castle Creek Road, and travel 10.7 miles to Express Creek Road and a small parking area on the left.

The ride

0.0 From Castle Creek Road go left on Express Creek Road over a bridge. Begin climbing up to a stream crossing.

0.8 Cross the stream and crank up a steep, short hill. Look right for great views up and down Castle Creek Valley. A few sections of level ground give brief relief from the climbing.

2.7 Cross over a stream and continue climbing on loose, rocky tread.

3.3 Level ground—what a surprise! Check out the great views and the alpine flowers in the summer months. Enjoy the level terrain—more climbing lies ahead.

4.0 Steep uphill. Keep those legs moving.

4.4 Express Creek Cutoff Trail goes off to the left. You continue straight across a bridge and get ready for

· Taylor Pass

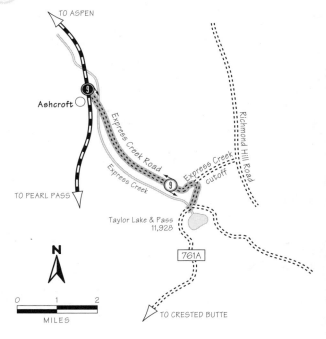

TO ASPEN

Ashcroft ○

⑨

Express Creek Road

Express Creek

⑨

Express Creek cutoff

Richmond Hill Road

TO PEARL PASS

Taylor Lake & Pass
11,928

761A

N

0   1   2
MILES

TO CRESTED BUTTE

the last big grunt (3+) to the top of Taylor Pass. The road takes a sharp right and cuts an impressive line to the top of Taylor Pass. The views to the north are nothing short of spectacular; if the hill doesn't take your breath away, the views will. Good spot to take a break.

5.5 Taylor Pass. Take in the view, then turn around and enjoy the downhill ride back.

11.0 Back at the parking area.

Taylor Pass to Crested Butte

Location: 11 miles south of downtown Aspen.

Distance: 27.6 miles one way.

Time: 5 to 8 hours.

Tread: Rough four-wheel road, singletrack, and double-track with a short section of paved road.

Aerobic level: Strenuous with a long climb to the top of Taylor Pass and then another climb up and over Star Pass. This is a huge ride that should only be attempted by strong intermediate or expert riders.

Technical difficulty: 2 to 4.

Hazards: Watch out for four-wheel traffic and motorcycle riders. This is a popular road during the summer months. Be prepared for sudden, violent weather changes and always expect snow on top of the pass. You should train at altitude before attempting this high-alpine ride. Bring lots of fluids and some energy bars—you'll need them.

Highlights: A great alpine bike tour that takes you up, over, and through some of Colorado's most spectacular alpine scenery. Spectacular views out to the Collegiate Peaks Range, alpine flowers in the summer months, and spectacular colors from the changing aspen in early fall.

Land status: White River National Forest.

Maps: USGS, Pitkin and Gunnison Counties.

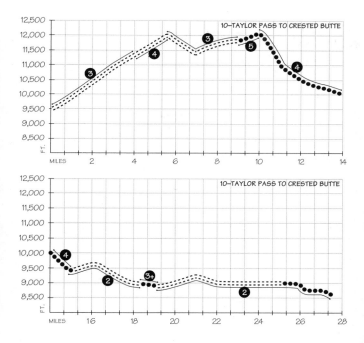

Access: From Main Street in Aspen travel west by bike or car on Colorado 82 to Maroon Creek Road. Go left on Maroon Creek Road for a short distance, make a quick left onto Castle Creek Road, and travel 10.7 miles to Express Creek Road and a small parking area on the left. The mileage starts from the junction of Castle Creek and Express Creek Roads.

The ride

0.0 From Castle Creek Road go left on Express Creek Road over a bridge. Begin climbing up to a stream crossing.

Taylor Pass to Crested Butte

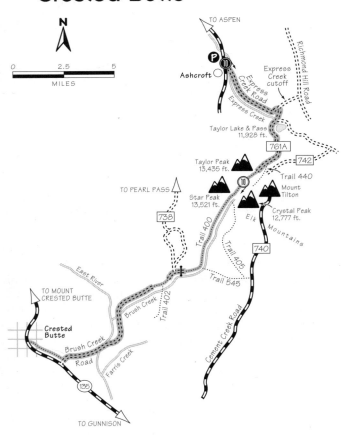

N

0   2.5   5
MILES

TO ASPEN

P **10**

Ashcroft

Richmond Hill Road

Express Creek cutoff

Express Creek Road

Express Creek

Taylor Lake & Pass
11,928 ft.

761A

742

Taylor Peak
13,435 ft.

Trail 440

10

Mount Tilton

TO PEARL PASS

Star Peak
13,521 ft.

Crystal Peak
12,777 ft.

738

Elk Mountains

Trail 400

Trail 405

740

East River

Trail 545

Brush Creek

Trail 402

Cement Creek Road

TO MOUNT CRESTED BUTTE

Crested Butte

Brush Creek Road

Farris Creek

135

TO GUNNISON

0.8 Cross the stream and crank up a steep, short hill. Look right for great views up and down Castle Creek Valley. A few sections of level ground give brief relief from the climbing.

2.7 Cross over a stream and continue climbing on loose, rocky tread.

3.3 Level ground—what a surprise! Check out the great views and the alpine flowers during the summer months. Enjoy the level terrain—more climbing lies ahead.

4.0 Steep uphill. Keep those legs moving.

4.4 Express Creek Cutoff Trail goes off to the left. You continue straight across a bridge and get ready for the last big grunt to the top of Taylor Pass. The road takes a sharp right and cuts an impressive line to Taylor Pass. The views to the north are nothing short of spectacular; if the hill doesn't take your breath away, the views will.

5.5 Taylor Pass.

6.0 Go right at a trail junction following Forest Road 761A. The road drops down and crosses over a small stream. Crank up a short hill to a trail junction. I hope you enjoy that downhill, because here comes another climb.

8.0 Trail 440 goes down to the left. You continue straight up a strenuous, rock-strewn hill.

9.3 Go left down the steep, tight trail. This is a great singletrack section with loads of wildflowers in the summer months.

10.3 Trail junction. Go up and to the right, following Trail 400. A short section of very steep riding (or in my case pushing) puts you on Star Pass.

10.7 Take a well-deserved rest. You earned it. The views are beautiful. Go right, down an awesome single-track trail. This is pure fun!

11.9 Trail 405 goes left. Continue straight and down a great singletrack run.

13.0 Cross over a small stream and follow the tight singletrack along East Brush Creek.

15.0 Arrive at a trail junction. The trail turns to doubletrack and you continue straight and down.

15.2 Trail junction. Continue straight and down into a dense, spruce forest. The trail becomes rocky and rooted in several sections. Watch your speed.

16.5 Pass through a gate; continue on more rocky tread.

16.9 Stream crossing—a big one.

17.1 Go left.

17.4 Another big stream crossing.

18.5 Go left on a tight singletrack trail high above Brush Creek. The trail is quite narrow and there are steep drop-offs to the left.

19.2 Back on the road. Farris Creek Trail is on your left. Continue straight down the road to a stream crossing.

19.5 Cross the stream and crank up a short hill.

20.2 Trail junction. Continue straight.

23.3 Brush Creek Trailhead. Continue straight up a slight uphill grade. Keep pumping toward Colorado 135.

25.6 Go right on Colorado 135. Look for a singletrack trail on the right. Hop on the trail and crank into mountain bike nirvana, Crested Butte.

27.6 Arrive at Crested Butte and the end of a great mountain bike ride.

Pearl Pass

Location: 14 miles south of downtown Aspen.

Distance: 11.4 miles out and back.

Time: 3 to 5 hours.

Tread: An extremely rough four-wheel-drive road.

Aerobic level: Strenuous with a 3,000-foot gain in altitude.

Technical difficulty: 2 to 4+.

Hazards: This is a serious, high-alpine ride. Be prepared for sudden, violent weather changes and snow on the road most of the year. Bring extra clothing, water, energy bars, and tubes in case of flats. More than likely you will be walking sections of this ride.

Highlights: The original, big-daddy, high-alpine ride in the Aspen area, with spectacular views of the Sawatch Range to

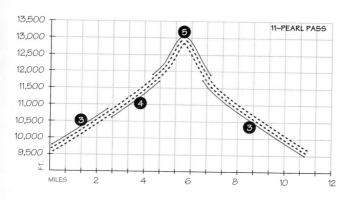

45

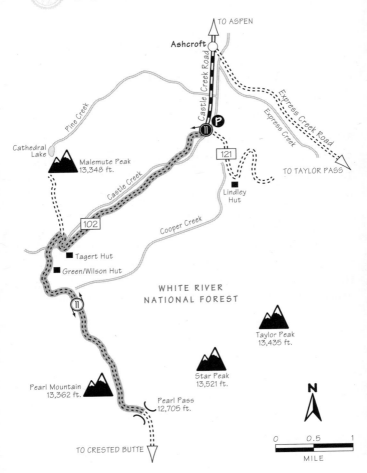

· Pearl Pass

TO ASPEN

Ashcroft

Castle Creek Road

Express Creek Road

Express Creek

TO TAYLOR PASS

Pine Creek

Cathedral Lake

Malemute Peak
13,348 ft.

Castle Creek

121

Lindley Hut

Cooper Creek

102

Tagert Hut

Green/Wilson Hut

WHITE RIVER
NATIONAL FOREST

Taylor Peak
13,435 ft.

Star Peak
13,521 ft.

Pearl Mountain
13,362 ft.

Pearl Pass
12,705 ft.

TO CRESTED BUTTE

N

0   0.5   1
MILE

the north and the San Juan Mountains a hundred miles to the south.

Land status: White River National Forest.

Maps: USGS, Pitkin County.

Access: From Main Street in Aspen travel west by bike or car on Colorado 82 to Maroon Creek Road. Go left on Maroon Creek Road for a short distance, make a quick left onto Castle Creek Road, and travel 13.4 miles to end of pavement and a small parking area on the right at the start of Forest Road 102. The mileage begins here.

The ride

0.0   From the parking area follow Forest Road 102 up toward Pearl Pass and Montezuma Basin. Don't be fooled by the gentle grade and easy riding.

0.6   Small reservoir on the right. Crank up a short, steep hill to a bridge over Castle Creek.

1.1   Cross over bridge and crank up a steep, loose, rocky hill. After the hill the trail continues to climb at a gentle grade to a creek crossing. The Toklat Ski Hut is on the right just before the creek crossing.

2.5   Cross over Castle Creek and crank up a series of short switchbacks to a road junction.

2.9   Montezuma Basin Road goes to the right. Continue left on the Pearl Pass Road. Things start to get serious here.

3.0   The Tagert and Green-Wilson Ski Huts are on the left. Begin a mile of hard riding on steep and loose (4) baby-head-size rocks. The air is thin, so don't feel bad about pushing.

4.2   The grade eases and you can actually ride this section. The views are just spectacular. Get ready for one last grunt to the top.

5.0 Steep riding on loose rock. You're almost there.

5.7 Top of Pearl Pass. Take a break and enjoy the alpine scenery before turning around and retracing your route back to the trailhead.

11.4 Back at your car. What a ride!

Government Trail East

Location: Snowmass Village.

Distance: 12.1 miles one way to Aspen, or a 19.6-mile loop in Snowmass.

Time: 2 to 4 hours.

Tread: 3.6 miles on paved roads, 1.2 miles on doubletrack, and 7.3 miles on singletrack.

Aerobic level: Moderate with a number of short, steep hills.

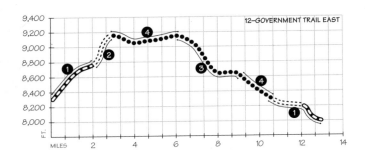

Technical difficulty: 4 on singletrack and 1 on the paved road and doubletrack.

Hazards: Watch out for car traffic on Wood Road and back in Aspen, and a lot of foot and bike traffic on summer weekends. There are some serious rock gardens, several water crossings, and steep, tight switchbacks.

Highlights: The most famous singletrack ride in the Aspen area, featuring a 7-mile stretch of excellent singletrack across the aspen-covered slopes of Snowmass and Buttermilk Ski Areas. Dropping a car in Aspen and shuttling back to Snowmass eliminates having to ride the bike path back up to Snowmass.

Land Status: White River National Forest and Pitkin County.

Maps: USGS, Pitkin County.

Access: From Aspen follow Colorado 82 toward Carbondale. Turn left up Brush Creek Road into Snowmass Village. Follow Brush Creek Road for 3 miles up to Wood Road. Go left on Wood Road and park in Base Lot A. The mileage starts from the intersection of Brush Creek Road and Wood Road.

The ride

0.0 Pedal up the paved Wood Road. A good warm-up.

1.6 Pass under a bridge.

2.2 Drop left down Elk Creek Road.

2.4 Come to a gate. Continue straight climbing up Elk Camp Road.

3.2 Arrive at a trail junction. The Government Trail goes east and west. You go left down the marked Government Trail to the east. Get ready for 7 miles of excellent singletrack riding.

· Government Trail East

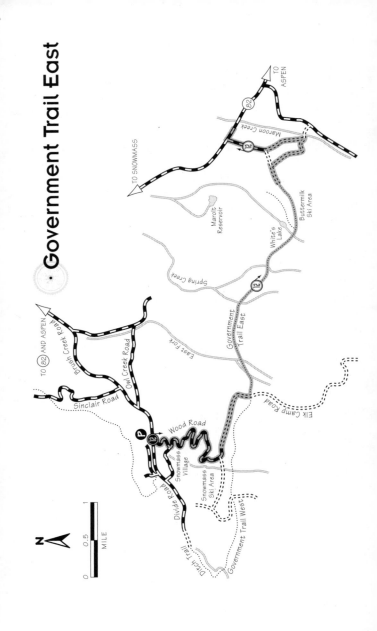

3.6 Sign with a grim warning and the first of several water (4) crossings.

4.3 Government Trail sign on the left.

4.8 The trail forks. Pedal right following excellent singletrack.

5.1 Stream crossing and wooden bridge. After the bridge, the trail shoots up a steep hill.

5.8 Gate and fence. Continue straight. There is some hard riding ahead.

6.7 Here comes some fun. The first of several streams and rock (4) gardens.

6.8 Gate on the left. Continue along the fenceline going down to a gate.

7.5 Orange gate. Continue straight through it.

7.8 The trail cuts across the Buttermilk Ski Area.

8.8 Water pipe on the right. Continue straight and down to a service road.

9.0 Cross the service road and follow singletrack on other side.

9.4 Roots, roots, and more roots (4). Drop down to a trail junction.

9.7 Go left on service road with Eagle Hill sign. Be on the lookout for singletrack trail on the right.

9.7 Go right on singletrack through a wooden gate.

10.3 Irrigation ditch and paved road. Go left down to Government Trail sign and singletrack trail with steep switchbacks (4) leading down to Maroon Creek.

10.7 Cross Maroon Creek on a bridge and go left along the creek up to the Bob Helms Bridge.

11.8 Bob Helms Bridge. Go left into Aspen (12.1 miles) or right following the bike path back to Snowmass.

19.6 Arrive back in Snowmass.

Government Trail West

Location: Snowmass Village.

Distance: 9.1-mile loop.

Time: 1 to 2.5 hours.

Tread: 3.6 miles on paved roads, 1.2 miles on doubletrack, and 4.3 miles on singletrack.

Aerobic level: Moderate with a number of short, steep hills.

Technical difficulty: 4 on singletrack and 1 on the paved road and doubletrack.

Hazards: Car traffic on Wood Road and tight, steep switchbacks on the descent to the Ditch Trail.

Highlights: An excellent ride, often overlooked for the more popular Government Trail East. Great singletrack riding, challenging hills, alpine flowers in the summer months, and brilliantly colored aspen in early fall.

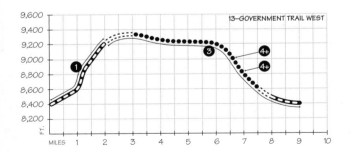

Land status: White River National Forest and Pitkin County.

Maps: USGS, Pitkin County.

Access: From Aspen follow Colorado 82 toward Carbondale. Turn left up Brush Creek Road into Snowmass Village. Follow Brush Creek Road for 3 miles up to Wood Road. Go left on Wood Road and park in Base Lot A. The mileage starts from the intersection of Brush Creek Road and Wood Road.

The ride

0.0 Pedal up the paved Wood Road. This paved section of the ride is an excellent warm-up that gets the blood flowing real quick.

1.6 Pass under a bridge.

2.2 Drop left down Elk Camp Road.

2.4 Come to a gate. Continue straight, climbing up Elk Camp Road.

3.2 Arrive at a trail junction. The Government Trail goes east and west. You go right up the steep, tight, (3) singletrack trail.

3.3 At the top of the hill, go right and down on tight singletrack.

3.7 The trail forks. Continue straight into the woods.

4.0 Cross over a small stream. Continue straight.

4.3 The trail cuts across a ski run and drops down to a stream crossing.

4.5 Pedal through the stream and crank up to a log bridge.

4.7 Crank over the log bridge and climb (3+) steeply up to a service road.

5.1 Drop down the road to a singletrack trail on the left.

· Government Trail West

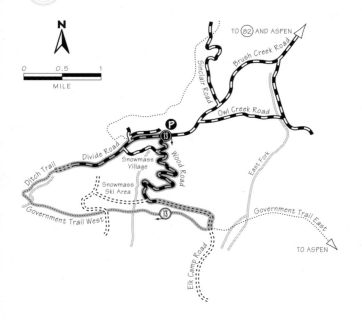

5.2 Go left on the well-marked Government Trail to Sam's Knob.

5.4 Trail junction. Continue straight on the Government Trail.

5.9 Hold on and get ready for a wild downhill run. Drop down the steep (4) switchbacks to the Ditch Trail.

6.5 Go right down the fast Ditch Trail. This is pure, mountain bike fun. Follow the smooth Ditch Trail to Divide Road.

7.7 Go right down the fast, paved Divide Road.

8.6 Go left.

9.1 Arrive back at the parking area.

14

Rim Trail

Location: Snowmass Village.

Distance: 6.5-mile loop.

Time: 1 to 1.5 hours.

Tread: 3.7 miles on singletrack, 1.5 miles on paved road, and 1.2 miles on gravel roads.

Aerobic level: Moderate with a steep climb to start the ride.

Technical difficulty: 3 on singletrack, 1 on paved and gravel road.

Hazards: Steep downhill sections with steep drop-offs; watch for other trail users and use caution. Be prepared for potentially violent afternoon storms on exposed ridge in summer months.

Highlights: One of the best singletrack rides in the Aspen area; fairly smooth tread with tight, twisting singletrack along a high ridgeline. Spectacular views up and down the Roaring Fork Valley.

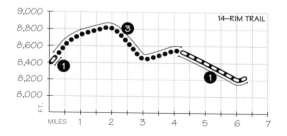

· Rim Trail

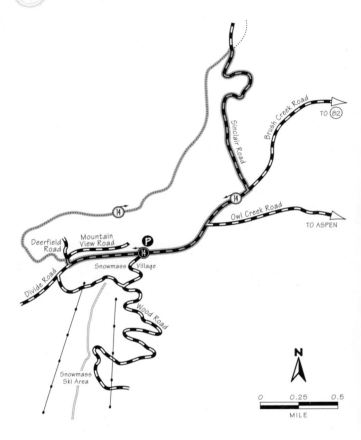

TO 82

TO ASPEN

Brush Creek Road

Sinclair Road

Owl Creek Road

14

14

P
14

Snowmass Village

Mountain
View Road

Deerfield
Road

Divide Road

Wood Road

Snowmass
Ski Area

N

0   0.25   0.5
MILE

Land status: White River National Forest and private.

Maps: USGS, Pitkin County.

Access: From Aspen follow Colorado 82 down the valley to the Snowmass Ski Area turnoff. Go left up Brush Creek Road for 3 miles to the intersection of Wood Road and Brush Creek Road. Park in the Base Lot A parking area.

The ride

0.0 Pedal up Divide Road.

0.4 Make a quick right onto Deerfield Road. Make a quick left onto the well-marked Rim Trail. Begin a steady climb up several switchbacks to reach the ridge at a fence line.

1.7 Arrive at a trail junction. Continue straight on tight singletrack.

2.0 The trail drops down a steep hill on tight, smooth singletrack. This is just pure fun.

2.9 Go left.

3.2 Climb up a short, steep hill to level ground.

3.6 Steep drop-offs to the right and great views out to the Roaring Fork Valley.

3.7 The trail forks; bear right and drop down to Sinclair Road.

4.2 Go right down Sinclair Road. Keep your speed in check down this fast road.

5.4 Brush Creek Road. Go right up to Divide Road and your car.

6.5 Back at the car. Go for another lap?

Woody Creek to Lendo

Location: 5 miles north of Aspen.

Distance: 16.4 miles out and back.

Time: 2 to 3 hours.

Tread: 9.8 miles on paved roads, 6.6 miles on dirt roads.

Aerobic level: Easy.

Technical difficulty: 2 on the dirt section.

Hazards: Car traffic.

Highlights: A great beginner's ride up a beautiful canyon following Woody Creek to the small town of Lendo. After the ride stop in the world-famous Woody Creek Tavern for good food and cool brews.

Land status: Pitkin County.

Maps: USGS, Pitkin County.

Access: From downtown Aspen go west on Colorado 82 for 5 miles to Woody Creek to the world-famous Woody Creek Tavern. The ride begins here.

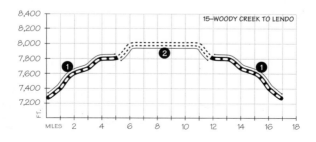

·Woody Creek to Lendo

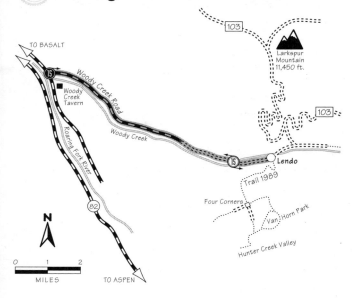

The ride

0.0 Head north from the Woody Creek Tavern to Woody
Creek Road.

0.3 Go right up Woody Creek Road.

3.2 Pass the Flying Dog Ranch.

3.9 Cross over a cattle guard.

4.9 The road turns to dirt and single-lane traffic. Use
caution on this section. The road parallels beautiful
Woody Creek as you climb gently to the old mining
town of Lendo.

8.2 Arrive at Lendo. Take a break and enjoy the scenery before turning around and retracing your route.

16.4 Back at the Woody Creek Tavern.

Forest Road 103

Location: 13 miles north of downtown Aspen.

Distance: 10 miles out and back.

Time: 1 to 2 hours.

Tread: Hard-packed dirt roads.

Aerobic level: Moderate with a good climb up to Larkspur Mountain.

Technical difficulty: 2 to 3.

Hazards: Four-wheel-drive traffic. Black flies in June.

Highlights: A great hill climb that leads to a number of other Forest Service roads and trails, with roadside wildflowers in summer and colorful aspen in fall.

Land status: White River National Forest.

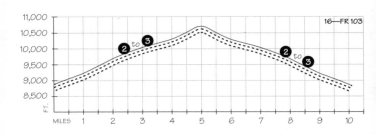

· Forest Road 103

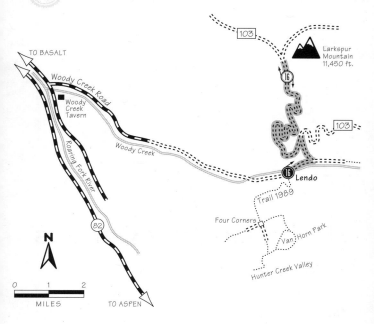

Maps: USGS, Pitkin County.

Access: From downtown Aspen go west on State Route 82 for 5 miles to Woody Creek. Follow Woody Creek Road for 8 miles to Lendo. Park your car on the right just past a bridge. The ride starts here.

The ride

0.0 From the parking area go right up Forest Road 103. Pass a mine on the right and begin to climb.

1.0 A trail goes right; you go left over Silver Creek.

1.5 The grade gets steep.

2.6 Great views out to Capitol Peak and the Maroon Bells.

3.0 Come to a road junction. Go right up past a gate. Keep an eye out for wildflowers in bloom.

4.2 The road curves right. Wildflowers are everywhere.

4.7 Spectacular views.

5.0 Arrive at the junction of Forest Roads 103 and 508. Take a break before retracing your route back to the parking area.

10.0 Back at your car.

Lendo to Four Corners

Location: 13 miles northeast of Aspen.

Distance: 5.4 miles.

Time: 1.5 to 2.5 hours.

Tread: 5.4 miles on singletrack.

Aerobic level: Strenuous with a pretty stiff climb up to Four Corners.

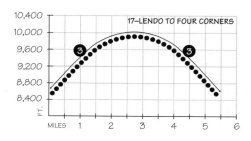

· Lendo to Four Corners

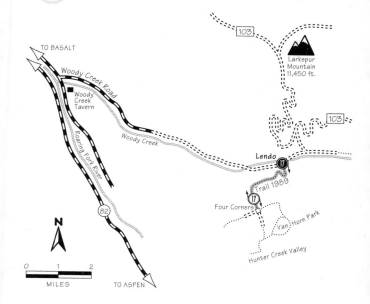

Technical difficulty: 3 on singletrack, 2 on the double-track section.

Hazards: Horse traffic, steep uphill climb, and other trail users.

Highlights: A great singletrack climb, with opportunities to explore the old mining town of Lendo and to hook up with other trails for a longer ride.

Land status: White River National Forest.

Maps: USGS, Pitkin County; Latitude 40, Aspen/Crested Butte Recreation Map.

Access: From downtown Aspen go west on Colorado 82 for 5 miles to Woody Creek. Follow Woody Creek Road for 8 miles to Lendo.

The ride

0.0 From the far end of town, look for a singletrack trail (marked Trail 1989) on the right leading into the woods. Follow the tight, rocky trail up past a mine. Continue climbing up to a small creek crossing.

1.0 Cross over the creek on very tight singletrack. Continue climbing.

1.7 Use caution on this tight singletrack section. Steep drop-offs to the right. Great views out to Larkspur Mountain.

2.1 The tread turns rocky (3) and becomes steeper. Power up to level tread.

2.2 Level tread. Continue straight up to Four Corners.

2.7 Arrive at Four Corners. Take a break before heading back. Keep your speed in check on the way down and be on the lookout for other trail users.

5.4 Back at Lendo.

Light Hill Road

Location: 12 miles south of downtown Aspen.

Distance: 7.6-mile loop.

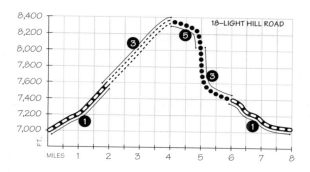

Time: 1 to 2 hours.

Tread: 3.9 miles on paved roads, 2.6 miles on doubletrack, and 1.1 miles on singletrack.

Aerobic level: Strenuous with a big climb up to the top of Light Hill Road.

Technical difficulty: 2 to 5. The descent off Light Hill Road is steep and loose, and can be quite dangerous.

Hazards: Use extreme caution on the downhill section and watch out for motorized traffic.

Highlights: A steep, lung-busting hill climb with incredible views to Snowmass Ski Area, Capitol Peak, and Mount Sopris, with a fun singletrack section near the end of the ride.

Land status: White River National Forest.

Maps: USGS, Pitkin County.

Access: From downtown Aspen go south on Colorado 82 for 12 miles to Snowmass Creek Road (not the Snowmass Ski Area). Follow Snowmass Creek Road for 1.7 miles to the junction of Capitol Creek and East Sopris Creek Roads. Park at the pullout on the left. The ride starts here.

· Light Hill Road

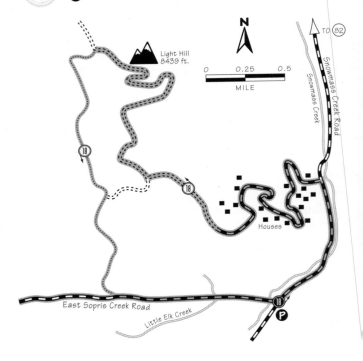

Light Hill 8439 ft.

N

0   0.25   0.5
MILE

Snowmass Creek Road

TO 82

Snowmass Creek

18

18

Houses

18

P

East Sopris Creek Road

Little Elk Creek

The ride

0.0 Head back down Snowmass Creek Road to Gateway Road.

0.4 Go left up Gateway Road and begin a long climb through a housing development.

1.6 Pedal right on Light Hill Road and follow up to where the pavement ends. Be on the lookout for bison.

2.3 Go straight up the steep, loose, dirt road. Crank hard up the small, steep hill. Drop down, then back up to a trail junction.

2.6 A jeep road goes to the left. You continue straight and up with great views to Capitol Peak.

2.7 The trail becomes steep and loose with baby-head-size river rocks in the road. The road bends to the right and it becomes difficult to pick a good line through the rocks. Keep cranking.

3.5 Steep switchbacks and spectacular views in all directions. Good spot to take a short break. Get ready for more steep climbing and loose tread ahead.

4.3 At the top. Don't go down the hill in front of you. Look to the left for an opening in the fenceline. Drop your seat and drop left through the fence going down a very loose, steep, rocky, over-the-handlebar hill. This is serious (5) stuff.

4.6 This is really serious stuff. Be careful!

4.8 Back to calmer waters.

4.9 Three-way junction. Go right down the singletrack trail. Make a left at a steep hill with doubletrack going up it. Drop down a short bit, then go right following the singletrack trail into scrub oak and sage.

5.6 The trail forks; go left on tight tread to a paved road.

6.0 Go left and fly down to a stop sign.

7.3 Go left at the stop sign and head back to your car.

7.6 Arrive back at the car.

Basalt Mountain Lower Loop

Location: 5 miles north of El Jebel.

Distance: 8.8-mile loop.

Time: 1 to 2 hours.

Tread: 4.4 miles on dirt roads and 4.4 miles on singletrack.

Aerobic level: Moderate with a couple of good climbs that keep the juices flowing.

Technical difficulty: 2 to 3.

Hazards: Four-wheel-drive traffic. This is a very popular area for hunters; use caution and wear bright clothing during the hunting seasons.

Highlights: A great introduction to the wonderful riding on and around Basalt Mountain. The singletrack riding is superb and ranks as some of the best in the Roaring Fork Valley. The hill climb up to the start of the singletrack is moderate with no technical difficulties. One of my favorite

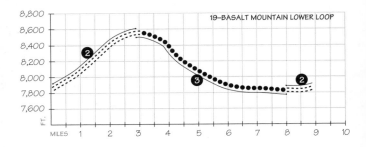

Basalt Mountain Lower Loop

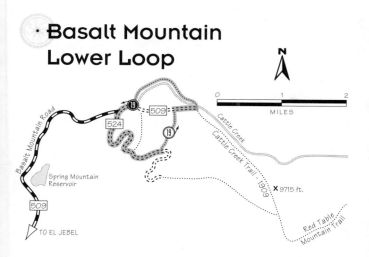

midvalley rides, with superb singletrack and moderate hill climbs.

Land status: White River National Forest.

Maps: USGS, Eagle County.

Access: From Aspen go down valley on Colorado 82 to El Jebel. Go right on Upper Cattle Creek Road for 5.3 miles to where the road forks. Go right on Forest Road 509 for 2.2 miles to the intersection of Forest Roads 509 and 524. Park at a large parking area on the right.

The ride

0.0 From the parking area follow Forest Road 524 up along the western flank of Basalt Mountain.

0.2 Gate. Continue straight up the smooth dirt road.

1.8 Pond on the left. Continue straight.

2.7 Arrive at a large, open meadow and a road junction. Continue up Forest Road 524.

2.9 Gate. Continue straight up Forest Road 524. Be on the lookout for a singletrack on the left diving into the forest.

3.4 Go left on the faint singletrack trail. Here's where the fun begins. Follow the tight, twisting singletrack down to a stream crossing.

4.4 Stream crossing. Continue straight through the dense pine and aspen forest.

5.0 Cross a creek and drop down to Forest Road 509.

5.3 Go right on Forest Road 509. Look for a singletrack trail on left.

5.5 Make a quick left onto the singletrack trail. Pedal up to a stream crossing,

5.9 Cross the stream. Go through a fence and pedal along the stream through several wet areas.

7.8 Pedal through the stream and head left on singletrack. Head back to Forest Road 509 near a log cabin.

8.1 Go right on Forest Road 509 up a short hill to a gate and the parking beyond.

8.8 Back at the parking area.

Basalt Mountain Upper Loop

Location: 5 miles north of El Jebel.

Distance: 14.6-mile loop.

Time: 2.5 to 4 hours.

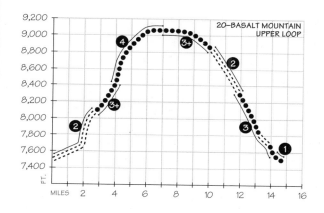

Tread: 5.5 miles on doubletrack and 9.1 miles on single-track.

Aerobic level: Strenuous with a long, steep climb up to the top of Basalt Mountain.

Technical difficulty: 2 to 4. Staying on the bike rates a solid 5.

Hazards: Four-wheel-drive traffic. This is a very popular area for hunters: use caution and wear bright clothing during the hunting seasons. This is a long, demanding, technical ride; bring a lot of water and some food. Weather can change quickly at this altitude; bring extra clothes. The trail can be a mud bath after heavy rains.

Highlights: A challenging ride even for expert cyclists, with a variety of trail surfaces and superb singletrack that is steep and technical on the uphill and fast downhill. Spectacular colors in early fall and wildflowers in summer.

Land status: White River National Forest.

Maps: USGS, Eagle County.

· Basalt Mountain
Upper Loop

Access: From Aspen go down valley on Colorado 82 to El Jebel. Go right on Upper Cattle Creek Road for 5.3 miles to where the road forks. Go right on Forest Road 509 for 2.2 miles to the intersection of Forest Roads 509 and 524. Park at a large parking area on the right.

The ride

0.0   From the parking area follow Forest Road 509 up to a gate.

0.2   Gate. Continue straight down the dirt road into a nice meadow.

0.6   Cattle guard and a cabin on the left.

0.7   Singletrack trail on the right. (Make a mental note, as you will be coming out on this trail at the end of the ride.) Continue straight on Forest Road 509.

1.2	Short, steep section up to a large open area with good camping spots.
2.2	Gate. Continue straight.
2.4	Herding pen and open meadow. Continue straight up to a gate.
2.6	Gate in front of you and another gate to your right. Go through the gate on the right, and onto Cattle Creek Trail 1909. The start of the trail can be very wet and muddy. Crank up a short, steep hill to a fenceline.
2.8	Go right up the tight, singletrack trail. Excellent singletrack (3+) riding through a forest of tall aspen and pine trees.
3.7	The first of two small stream crossings.
4.0	Rocky, rooted, and loose tread (4). The start of a steep climb.
4.4	The grade eases for a moment. Keep cranking hard. This is fun stuff.
5.0	The trail slices through a meadow. Enjoy—there is some hard riding ahead.
5.5	Hill—a big one. Pedal, push, or be pushed up a series of steep (5-) switchbacks to level ground. Take notice of the large, scree slope off to the right. Almost at the top now.
6.4	Level ground. Continue straight into a beautiful, open meadow.
6.6	Trail junction. Red Table Mountain Trail goes straight into a beautiful meadow. You go right onto the Basalt Mountain Trail.
7.2	Nice downhill run through an open meadow.
7.8	Cow pond on the right. Continue straight down on tight, singletrack tread.
8.3	Gate. Continue straight.
8.4	Three-way junction. Go right, down the wide trail through some very rocky (3+) tread.

9.5   Trail junction. Go right and up through a clear-cut.

10.0   Gate. Go right and down Forest Road 524. The riding is very fast; watch out for car traffic.

12.0   Go right on the Basalt Mountain Lower Loop Trail. This is great singletrack riding.

13.0   Pedal through a small stream.

13.6   Pedal through a larger stream and crank down the tight singletrack to Forest Road 509.

13.9   Go left up Forest Road 509.

14.6   Arrive back at the parking area.

Red Hill

Location: Carbondale.

Distance: 6.1-mile loop.

Time: 1 to 2 hours.

Tread: 2.8 miles on paved and dirt roads and 3.3 miles on singletrack.

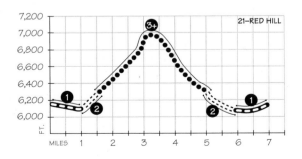

Aerobic level: Moderate with a good climb up to the top of Red Hill.

Technical difficulty: 2 to 4 on the singletrack, 1 to 2 on road and doubletrack.

Hazards: Car traffic and other trail users. This popular trail sees heavy use on most weekends during the spring, summer, and fall months.

Highlights: A well-maintained trail with beautiful single-track and great views of Mount Sopris and the Roaring Fork Valley; good for a quick workout, with the option of doing laps for more mileage or reversing direction for variety.

Land status: BLM.

Maps: USGS, Garfield County.

Access: The intersection of Colorado 133 and Main Street in Carbondale. The mileage starts here.

The ride

0.0 Travel north on Colorado 133.

1.0 Traffic light and intersection with Colorado 82. Use caution and pedal straight across Colorado 82 to Red Hill Road. Follow Red Hill Road uphill to a trail junction on the left.

1.4 Go left along the road on the Gulch Trail. Crank on tight tread up a small gulch going away from the road.

1.5 Steep switchbacks (3+) on tight tread go uphill into the trees—this is awesome riding.

2.1 Short, rock (4) steps.

2.4 A steep, strenuous hill up tight switchbacks leads to level ground and a trail junction.

2.7 Go right onto wonderful singletrack. This is just what the bike doctor ordered. Follow the tight, winding singletrack up toward the top of Red Hill.

⦾ Red Hill

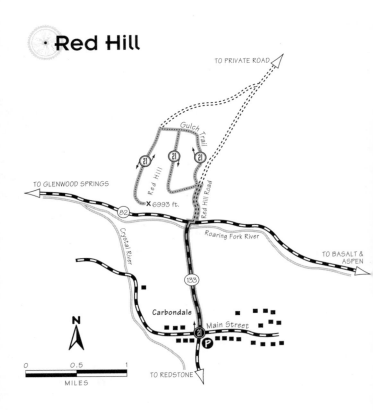

TO PRIVATE ROAD

Gulch Trail

21

21

21

Red Hill

Red Hill Road

TO GLENWOOD SPRINGS

X 6993 ft.

82

Roaring Fork River

Crystal River

TO BASALT & ASPEN

133

Carbondale

21 Main Street

P

N

0   0.5   1

MILES

TO REDSTONE

3.1 Steep (3+), loose, and rocky hill. Crank hard and you'll be at the top.

3.2 The top of Red Hill. Fantastic views out to Mount Sopris and Roaring Fork Valley. Turn around and head back to the Gulch Trail.

3.7 Don't go left on the Gulch Trail. Continue straight on tight, twisting singletrack through and around the trees across the side of Red Hill.

4.0 The trail drops steeply down some tight switchbacks and rock steps.

- **4.2** Head up and to the right on tight singletrack. The trail makes a sharp left down along the East Ridge of Red Hill. This is cool stuff.
- **4.5** A BLM kiosk. Go left down the steep hill to Red Hill Road.
- **4.7** Red Hill Road. Do another lap, do the same ride in reverse, or head back to Carbondale.
- **6.1** Back at Main Street.

Thompson Creek Road

Location: Carbondale.

Distance: 15.2 miles out and back.

Time: 1.5 to 2.5 hours.

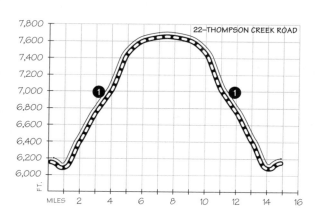

· Thompson Creek Road

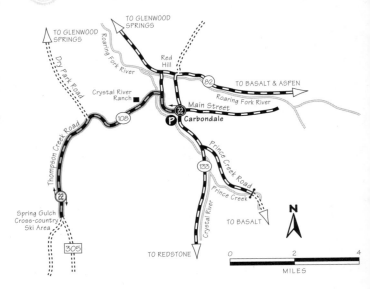

Tread: 15.2 miles on paved road.

Aerobic level: Moderate with a steady climb up to Forest Road 305 (the turn-around point).

Technical difficulty: 1.

Hazards: Car traffic.

Highlights: A great early-spring ride, with a good climb and great views to Mount Sopris and the Roaring Fork Valley.

Land status: Garfield County.

Maps: USGS, Garfield County.

Access: The intersection of Colorado 133 and Main Street in Carbondale. The mileage starts here.

The ride

0.0 Go right on Main Street away from downtown and toward the Colorado Mountain School and the Crystal River.

0.9 Bridge over the Crystal River. Continue straight up the steep hill.

2.3 The Crystal River Ranch. Steady climb ahead up to Dry Park Road.

4.0 Dry Park Road on the right. Continue straight.

5.2 Moderate hill climb. Continue straight.

7.1 Spring Gulch Cross Country Ski Area on the right.

7.6 The road forks, with Forest Road 305 going down to the left. Take a rest before turning around and retracing your route back to Carbondale.

15.2 Arrive back at Colorado 133 and Main Street.

Lake Ridge Lakes

Location: 8 miles south of Carbondale.

Distance: 19.4 miles out and back.

Time: 2.5 to 4 hours.

Tread: 2 miles on singletrack and 17.4 miles on double-track and jeep roads.

Aerobic level: Strenuous with a continuous grunt up Forest Road 306 and a steep climb on tight singletrack up to the lakes.

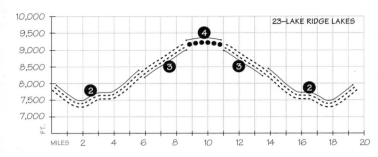

Technical difficulty: 2 to 3 on the doubletrack and jeep roads, and 3 to 4 on the singletrack.

Hazards: Hunters (in season) and jeep traffic. Fast downhill with several tight turns and steep drop-offs. Don't do this ride after a rainstorm; the road and trail turn to a thick, gooey playdough that sticks to your bike and turns it into a hundred-pound monster.

Highlights: An amazing, rugged mountain ride that gains almost 2,000 feet in a 4-mile climb; beautiful Lake Ridge Lakes offer opportunities to view wildlife and fish for cutthroat trout; stunning early fall colors.

Land status: Garfield County.

Maps: USGS, Garfield County, Pitkin County, and Gunnison County.

Access: From the intersection of Colorado 133 and Main Street in Carbondale, go right on Main Street, which soon turns into Thompson Creek Road (County Road 108). Follow Thompson Creek Road for 7.6 miles to Forest Road 305 just past the Spring Gulch Cross Country Ski Area. The mileage starts from the parking area at Forest Road 305.

Lake Ridge Lakes

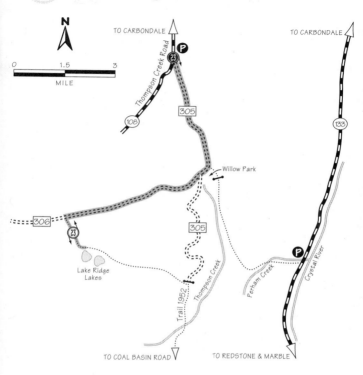

The ride

0.0   Follow Forest Road 305 down to Thompson Creek. There are some tight turns; be on the lookout for bovines on the road.

2.2   Great camping spots along Thompson Creek.

2.5   Cross over Thompson Creek and begin climbing.

3.5   Top of the hill. Drop down to a road junction.

3.9   The road splits. Forest Road 305 goes down and left into Willow Park. Forest Road 306 goes straight. You follow Forest Road 306 and begin a steady, 4-mile climb up to Lake Ridge.

4.9   Mile marker 1 on the right. Great views of Assignation Ridge to the left.

5.9   Mile marker 2.

6.0   Steep hill leads up to a stream crossing.

6.3   Pedal through a stream and climb steeply through some switchbacks.

6.7   Gate. Continue straight and up through a beautiful aspen forest.

7.4   Short, steep section.

7.6   This is the last steep climb.

7.8   Level ground at an open meadow. Take a short break. Continue straight and drop down to another large, open meadow.

8.6   Go left into the meadow on doubletrack tread.

8.7   Go left across a small stream up to a red gate and singletrack trail. Pedal through the gate and begin a mile of continuous climbing on tight, twisting singletrack through a beautiful aspen forest. There are several log (4+) jumps on this section.

9.7   Lake Ridge Lakes are on the right. Leave your bike here and climb up a short hill to the lakes. Take a long break and enjoy the serenity. Turn around and retrace your route back to the parking area.

19.4   Arrive back at the parking area.

24

Tall Pines

Location: 8 miles south of Carbondale.

Distance: 17.9 miles point to point.

Time: 2.5 to 4 hours.

Tread: 6.8 miles on singletrack, 8.5 miles on doubletrack, and 2.6 miles on paved road.

Aerobic level: Strenuous with a lot of climbing.

Technical difficulty: 2 to 3 on the doubletrack and jeep roads, and 3 to 4 on the singletrack.

Hazards: Hunters in season and jeep traffic. Be on the lookout for four-wheel-drive traffic and bovines along the road and trail.

Highlights: An excellent, varied ride featuring open meadows, stream crossings, views to Mount Sopris, great singletrack, fast downhills, and solitude.

Land status: Garfield County.

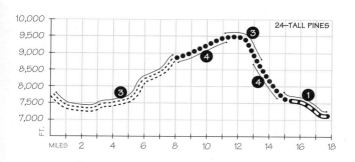

• Tall Pines

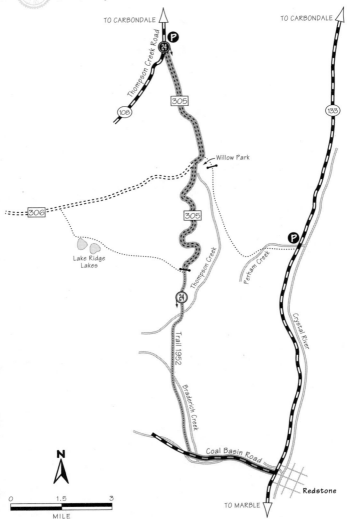

TO CARBONDALE

TO CARBONDALE

Thompson Creek Road

P

24

305

108

Willow Park

305

306

Thompson Creek

Lake Ridge
Lakes

24

Perham Creek

P

Crystal River

Trail 1952

Braderich Creek

Coal Basin Road

Redstone

TO MARBLE

133

N

0   1.5   3
MILE

Maps: USGS, Garfield County, Pitkin and Gunnison Counties.

Access: From the intersection of Colorado 133 and Main Street in Carbondale, go right on Main Street, which soon turns to Thompson Creek Road (County Road 108). Follow Thompson Creek Road for 7.6 miles to Forest Road 305 just past the Spring Gulch Cross Country Ski Area. The mileage starts at Forest Road 305. The best way to do this ride is with a car shuttle, which eliminates the road riding. Leave a car in Redstone and one at the trailhead.

The ride

0.0 Follow Forest Road 305 down to Thompson Creek. There are some tight turns; be on the lookout for bovines on the road.

2.2 Great camping spots along Thompson Creek.

2.5 Cross over Thompson Creek and begin climbing.

3.5 Top of the hill. Drop down to a road junction.

3.9 The road splits. Forest Road 305 goes down and left, Forest Road 306 goes straight. Follow Forest Road 305 into Willow Park.

4.5 Cross over Thompson Creek. Climb up a steep hill to Parsnip Flats. Great views of Assignation Ridge and Mount Sopris to the left.

5.5 Arrive at a trail junction, signed for South Thompson Creek and Coal Creek. Continue left.

6.3 The road forks; continue straight.

6.8 Gate across the road. Continue straight.

7.4 Intersection at a large meadow. Continue left down the faint doubletrack trail. Begin climbing into and out of several drainages.

8.0 Pedal through the drainage and (4) go up and to the right.

8.5 Trail junction. Go through the gate following South Thompson Trail 1952.

9.1 Stream crossing.

9.5 Pass through a gate at a fenceline. The trail follows the fenceline and then goes right to a stream crossing. Crank for all you're worth up a steep, steep hill. Several steep hills lie ahead.

11.2 Cross the creek and begin an extended climb on rocky and rooted tread.

12.2 Arrive at the top of the hill and long log fence. Here's the reward for all that hard work: downhill single-track.

13.2 Cross a small drainage.

13.6 Cross Braderich Creek in a large, open meadow. Go right after crossing the creek. This is just incredible riding; enjoy.

14.4 Trail junction. Continue straight down to a fence-line.

15.1 Caution: Drop down a series of steep, tight switch-backs to Forest Road 307.

15.3 Go left down Forest Road 307.

17.9 Arrive at Colorado 133 and the town of Redstone.

Prince Creek Road

Location: Carbondale.

Distance: 15.4 miles out and back.

Time: 1 to 3 hours.

Tread: Hard-packed dirt roads.

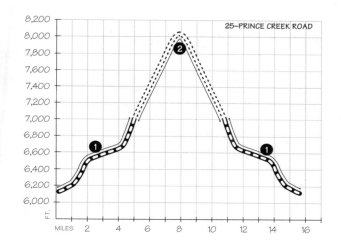

Aerobic level: Easy with a moderate climb up to Dinkle Lake Road.

Technical difficulty: 1 to 2.

Hazards: Car traffic on Colorado 133 and Prince Creek Road.

Highlights: A nice ride that gets you on some dirt, with mountain views close to town.

Land status: White River National Forest.

Maps: USGS, Pitkin County.

Access: The intersection of Colorado 133 and Main Street in Carbondale. The mileage starts here.

The ride

0.0 Follow Colorado 133 toward Mount Sopris and the town of Redstone.

Prince Creek Road

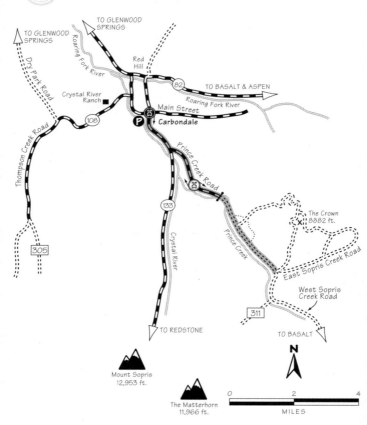

TO GLENWOOD SPRINGS

TO GLENWOOD SPRINGS

Red Hill

Roaring Fork River

TO BASALT & ASPEN

82

Roaring Fork River

Dry Park Road

Crystal River Ranch

Main Street

108

25

P

Carbondale

Thompson Creek Road

Prince Creek Road

25

The Crown
8882 ft.

133

Prince Creek

305

East Sopris Creek Road

Crystal River

West Sopris Creek Road

311

TO REDSTONE

TO BASALT

N

Mount Sopris
12,953 ft.

The Matterhorn
11,966 ft.

0   2   4

MILES

1.7 Go left on Prince Creek Road. Follow Prince Creek Road past a red barn and beautiful rolling farmlands, climbing gently.

4.6 The road turns to dirt; Prince Creek is on the right.

5.0 Cross over a cattleguard.

6.2 A road goes left to the Porcupine Loop Trail. Continue straight up Prince Creek Road.

7.2 Arrive at the top of Prince Creek Road. Take a rest, then retrace your route back to Carbondale.

15.4 Back at Main Street.

Porcupine Loop

Location: Carbondale.

Distance: 14.0-mile loop.

Time: 1 to 2 hours.

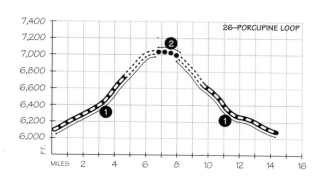

Porcupine Loop

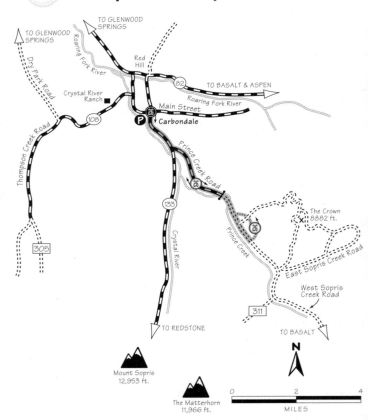

TO GLENWOOD SPRINGS

TO GLENWOOD SPRINGS

Roaring Fork River

Red Hill

Dry Park Road

82

TO BASALT & ASPEN

Crystal River Ranch

Roaring Fork River

Main Street

26

P

Carbondale

Thompson Creek Road

108

Prince Creek Road

26

The Crown 8882 ft.

305

133

Crystal River

Prince Creek

26

East Sopris Creek Road

West Sopris Creek Road

311

TO REDSTONE

TO BASALT

N

Mount Sopris 12,953 ft.

The Matterhorn 11,966 ft.

0   2   4
MILES

Tread: 1.1 miles on singletrack, 8.8 miles on paved roads, and 4.1 miles on dirt roads and doubletrack trails.

Aerobic level: Easy. There are a couple of short hills on good tread.

Technical difficulty: 2 to 3 on the singletrack section, 1 for rest of ride.

Hazards: Watch out for car traffic. Don't do this ride after a rain or snowstorm; the road and trail become a mess once wet.

Highlights: A great novice ride with varying terrain, short hills, and no real technical difficulty; access to other riding trails; one of the first rides to dry out in spring.

Land status: BLM.

Maps: USGS, Garfield County.

Access: The ride begins at the intersection of Colorado 133 and Main Street in Carbondale. The mileage starts here.

The ride

0.0 Follow Colorado 133 toward Mount Sopris and the town of Redstone.

1.7 Go left on Prince Creek Road. Follow Prince Creek Road past a red barn and beautiful rolling farmlands, climbing gently.

4.6 The road turns to dirt; Prince Creek is on the right.

5.0 Cross over a cattleguard.

6.2 Make a sharp left going past a gate and kiosk.

6.7 Go left onto a tight singletrack trail. Here's where the fun begins. Enjoy a mile of tight, twisting singletrack riding.

7.8 Go left down the rocky four-wheel-drive road to Prince Creek Road.

8.3 Go right on Prince Creek Road and retrace your route back to Carbondale.

14.0 Arrive back in Carbondale.

The Crown

Location: 5 miles northwest of Carbondale.

Distance: 10.7-mile loop.

Time: 2 to 3 hours.

Tread: 1.1 miles on singletrack and 9.6 miles on dirt roads and doubletrack trails.

Aerobic level: Strenuous. The first 3.5 miles are uphill; the last mile of the climb is extremely steep and arduous.

Technical difficulty: 5 on the doubletrack and 3 on the singletrack.

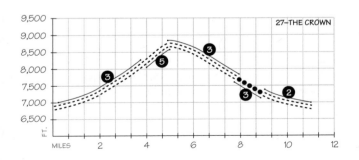

Hazards: You are going to push your bike on the last up-hill section. Use caution on the very fast downhill with its sharp turns and loose tread.

Highlights: A great ride that offers spectacular views of several Colorado natural landmarks; brilliant colors in fall and wildflowers in summer; serious uphill section; southern exposure makes this ride one of the first to dry out in the spring.

Land status: BLM.

Maps: USGS, Mesa County.

Access: From Colorado 133 and Main Street in Carbondale, ride or drive south on Colorado 133 for 1.7 miles to Prince Creek Road. Turn left and follow Prince Creek Road for 2.9 miles to a pullout/parking area where the road turns to dirt. The mileage starts here.

The ride

0.0 Pedal up Prince Creek Road.

1.2 Porcupine Loop Trail goes sharply to the left. You continue straight.

1.7 Large parking area on the right.

2.2 The road becomes steep.

2.7 Great views out to Mount Sopris on the right.

2.9 Pedal over a cattleguard.

3.0 Dinkle Lake Road and access to the Thomas Lake Trailhead goes right; you continue straight.

3.1 Go left into a large parking area. Here is where the fun begins. Crank up the steep, loose hill over some berms.

3.4 Hit a level area. Go left up the really steep, loose hill. It is hard enough just to push your bike through this section.

• The Crown

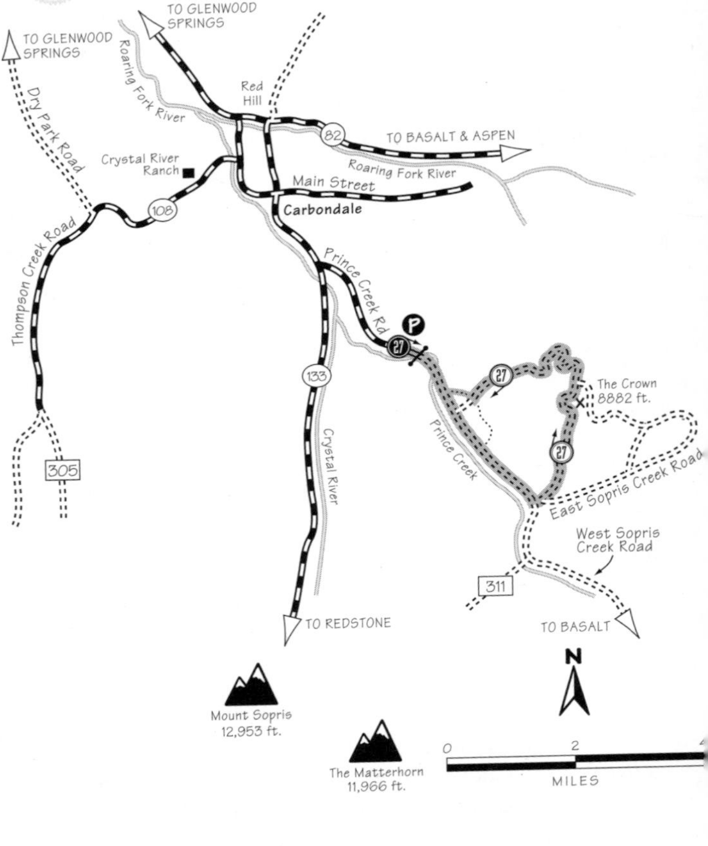

TO GLENWOOD
SPRINGS

TO GLENWOOD
SPRINGS

Roaring Fork River

Red
Hill

82

TO BASALT & ASPEN

Roaring Fork River

Crystal River
Ranch

Main Street

Carbondale

Dry Park Road

108

Thompson Creek Road

Prince Creek Rd

P
27

27

The Crown
8882 ft.

305

133

27

Prince Creek

East Sopris Creek Road

Crystal River

West Sopris
Creek Road

311

TO REDSTONE

TO BASALT

N

Mount Sopris
12,953 ft.

The Matterhorn
11,966 ft.

0   2

MILES

3.5 Drop down a short hill. Be on the lookout for wild-flowers.

3.7 Another steep hill. Crank hard!

4.0 The grade eases for the moment. Enjoy!

4.3 One more steep little hill.

4.5 The top. You made it! Take a well-deserved rest and enjoy the panoramic views. Drop down a steep hill.

5.3 Cross over a cattleguard.

5.8 Another cattleguard and a trail junction. Continue straight down the fast downhill run.

6.7 Make a sharp left, still going downhill.

8.7 Make a sharp right onto the Porcupine Loop Trail. Enjoy a mile of tight, twisting singletrack.

9.8 Trail junction. Make a sharp left and head down loose, rocky tread.

10.2 Go left.

10.3 Go right down Prince Creek Road.

10.7 Arrive back at the car. Bust out a cold one—you deserve it.

Thomas Lakes

Location: 10 miles south of Carbondale.

Distance: 7.6 miles out and back.

Time: 1 to 2.5 hours.

Tread: 4.0 miles on singletrack and 3.6 miles on double-track.

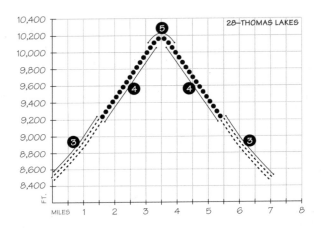

Aerobic level: Strenuous. There is a good 1.5-mile climb up to the Thomas Lakes Trail, and the last mile to the lakes will test the lungs, legs, and skills of most cyclists.

Technical difficulty: Very short section of 5 on the single-track; overall the rating is 4, with sections of 3 on the doubletrack.

Hazards: This is a very popular trail; keep your speed in check and yield to horseback riders. Use caution on the fast, loose, rocky downhill back to the parking area.

Highlights: A technical ride that will test the skills of most expert riders. Take a break and enjoy the two beautiful alpine lakes neatly tucked below the impressive summit of Mount Sopris.

Land status: White River National Forest.

Maps: USGS, Garfield County.

Thomas Lakes

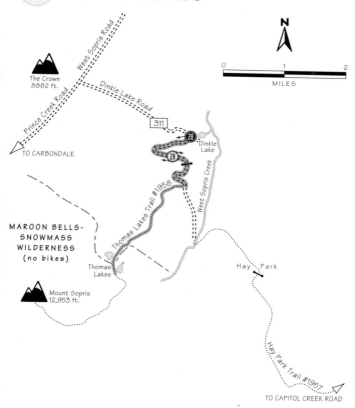

The Crown
8882 ft.

West Sopris Road

Prince Creek Road

Dinkle Lake Road

N

0   1   2
MILES

TO CARBONDALE

311

28

Dinkle
Lake

28

West Sopris Creek

Thomas Lakes Trail #1958

MAROON BELLS-
SNOWMASS
WILDERNESS
(no bikes)

Thomas
Lakes

Mount Sopris
12,953 ft.

Hay Park

Hay Park Trail #1957

TO CAPITOL CREEK ROAD

Access: From the intersection of Main Street and Colorado
133 in Carbondale, go south on Colorado 133 for 1.7 miles
to Prince Creek Road. Go left on Prince Creek Road for 7
miles to Dinkle Lake Road. Turn right on Dinkle Lake Road
and travel 1.4 miles to a large parking area on the left and
the Thomas Lakes Trailhead.

The ride

0.0 From the parking area, follow the Thomas Lakes Trail up past a kiosk. The trail bends to the right and climbs steadily.

0.6 Steep, rocky (3) tread. Continue cranking and keep those legs moving.

0.9 More steep (3) climbing over baby-head-size rocks.

1.2 The trail breaks out of the trees and views appear to the north and east.

1.3 Arrive at a gate. Go through the gate and climb up a short, steep hill. The tread becomes level and views surround you in all directions.

1.8 Arrive at a trail junction. The Hay Park Trail goes straight. You go up and right on the Thomas Lakes Trail. The trail is tight and steep. Crank up a very steep hill. Most cyclists will push through this section.

2.1 Open meadow with views extending in all directions. Enjoy this mostly flat section; things turn ugly real quick.

2.2 Steep rocky tread. Get ready for a mile of continuous rock hopping and steep hills.

3.2 Relief, for the moment.

3.4 The start of a very steep, loose, rock-infested hill (solid 5). Crank for all you are worth and then some.

3.6 Level ground. Take a breather and continue straight up.

3.8 Arrive at Thomas Lakes. Take a well-deserved rest and enjoy the lakes and the scenery before turning around and retracing your route back to the parking area.

7.6 Arrive back at your car.

29

Hay Park

Location: 10 miles south of Carbondale.

Distance: 8.8 miles out and back.

Time: 1 to 2 hours.

Tread: 5.0 miles on singletrack and 3.8 miles on double-track.

Aerobic level: Moderate. There is a good 1.5-mile climb up to the Thomas Lakes Trail.

Technical difficulty: 4 on the singletrack section and 2 on the doubletrack.

Hazards: This is a very popular trail; keep your speed in check and yield to horseback riders. Use caution on the fast, loose, rocky downhill back to the parking area.

Highlights: A fantastic, highly scenic ride with awesome singletrack, summer wildflowers, and spectacular fall foliage.

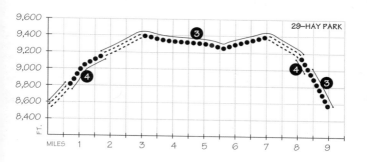

Land status: White River National Forest.

Maps: USGS, Garfield County.

Access: From the intersection of Main Street and Colorado 133 in Carbondale, go south on Colorado 133 for 1.7 miles to Prince Creek Road. Go left on Prince Creek Road for 7 miles to Dinkle Lake Road. Turn right on Dinkle Lake Road and travel 1.4 miles to a large parking area on the right and the Thomas Lakes Trailhead.

The ride

0.0   From the parking area, follow the Thomas Lakes Trail up past a kiosk. The trail bends to the right and climbs steadily.

0.6   Steep, rocky (3) tread. Continue cranking and keep those legs moving.

0.9   More steep (3) climbing over baby-head-size rocks.

1.2   The trail breaks out of the trees and views appear to the north and east.

1.3   Arrive at a gate. Go through the gate and climb up a short, steep hill. The tread becomes level and views surround you in all directions.

1.8   Arrive at a trail junction. The Thomas Lakes Trail goes off to the right. You continue straight on the Hay Park Trail.

2.1   Trail breaks out into an open meadow surrounded by beautiful aspen trees.

2.4   Cow pond on the left. Continue straight.

2.7   Trail turns to singletrack and climbs gently.

3.0   Pedal across West Sopris Creek, climbing up into a dense spruce forest.

3.6   The trail becomes tight singletrack in a large open meadow filled with wildflowers and bovines.

· Hay Park

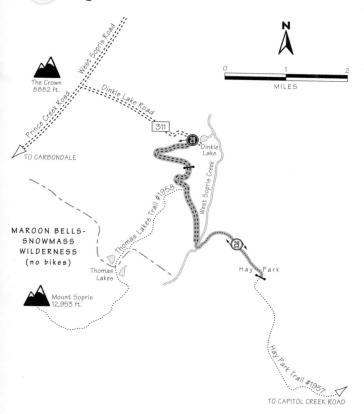

3.7 Crank over a small bridge and climb on tight, rutted singletrack up to a fenceline.

4.1 Fenceline and cattleguard. Continue straight over cattleguard down into Hay Park. The views to Capitol Peak are amazing. It doesn't get much better than this!

4.4 The turnaround point. Take a break and enjoy the scenery.

8.8 Arrive back at the parking area.

[Note: You can easily turn this ride into an extended tour by continuing straight on the Hay Park Trail on wonderful singletrack to Capitol Creek Road. Go left on Capitol Creek Road down to East Sopris Creek Road. Go left on East Sopris Creek Road to West Sopris Creek Road. Go left up West Sopris Creek Road to Prince Creek Road and Dinkle Lake Road. Go left on Dinkle Lake Road to the parking area. Total distance: thirty miles.]

Perham Creek

Location: 10 miles south of Carbondale.

Distance: 9.0 miles out and back.

Time: 1 to 2.5 hours.

Tread: 8.2 miles on singletrack, 0.8 mile on doubletrack.

Aerobic level: The initial climb is very strenuous with steep, rocky tread for the first 2 miles.

Technical difficulty: Staying on the bike for the ride would rate a 5 on the singletrack section, 2 to 3 on the doubletrack.

Hazards: There are some very technical sections on rough tread. The downhill back to the trailhead is difficult; use caution. Be on the lookout for other trail users.

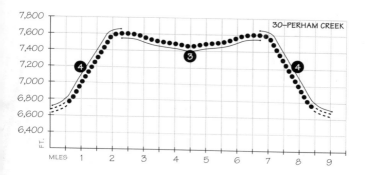

Highlights: A great ride and a real challenge for the expert mountain cyclist. Features beautiful scenery and great views.

Land status: White River National Forest.

Maps: USGS, Pitkin County.

Access: From the intersection of Colorado 133 and Main Street in Carbondale, follow Colorado 133 toward Redstone. Travel 10.2 miles to a pullout/parking area on the right. A sign marks Perham Creek Trail 1949.

The ride

0.0 Climb along Perham Creek. The climb is steep and unrelenting for the first mile.

0.9 Momentary relief from the climbing.

1.2 Pedal under a large rock tower. Beyond the tower the trail is steep, rocky, and full of roots.

1.3 Cross over a small drainage.

2.1 The trail pulls away from Perham Creek and heads toward Assignation Ridge.

2.3 Pass through a large, open meadow with beautiful aspen trees.

· Perham Creek

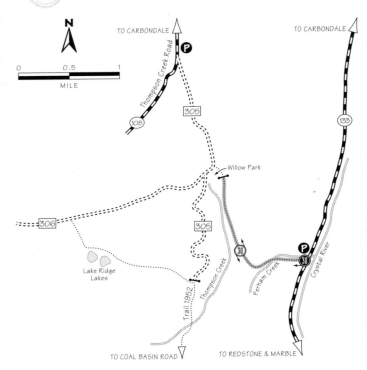

2.6 Trail junction. Go left on singletrack. Here's where the fun begins. Enjoy an extended downhill run on excellent singletrack.

3.3 Follow singletrack on the right (east) side of Thompson Creek to a large meadow. Follow the trail to a barbed wire fence and gate.

4.5 Arrive at gate. Take a long break. Turn around and retrace your route back to the trailhead.

9.0 Arrive (hopefully in one piece) back at the trailhead.

Lead King Basin/Lost Trail Creek

Location: 28 miles south of Carbondale.

Distance: 16.1-mile loop.

Time: 2.5 to 5 hours.

Tread: Doubletrack and rough jeep roads.

Aerobic level: Moderate to strenuous with a long climb in and out of Lead King Basin.

Technical difficulty: 1 to 3.

Hazards: A high-altitude ride with some steep climbs and rough tread. Be prepared for sudden weather changes.

Highlights: A sensational alpine mountain bike adventure on four-wheel-drive roads featuring magnificent scenery—bring a camera and lots of film.

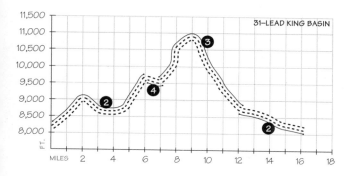

· Lead King Basin/Lost Trail Creek

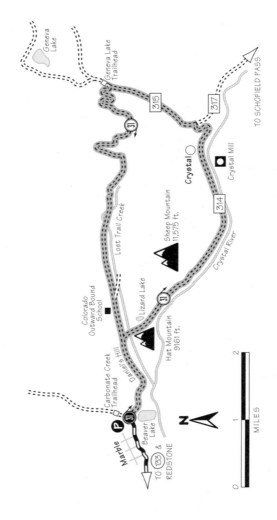

Geneva Lake

Geneva Lake Trailhead

315

31

317

TO SCHOFIELD PASS

Lost Trail Creek

Crystal

314

Crystal Mill

Sheep Mountain
11,575 ft.

Crystal River

Colorado
Outward Bound
School

Lizard Lake

31

Daniel's Hill

Carbonate Creek
Trailhead

Hat Mountain
9161 ft.

Marble

31

P

Beaver Lake

133

TO 133 &
REDSTONE

N

0   1   2

MILES

Land status: White River National Forest.

Maps: USGS, Pitkin County.

Access: From the intersection of Colorado 82 and Colorado 133 in Carbondale, follow 133 to the Marble turnoff. Travel 6 miles through the town of Marble to a parking area on the right at Beaver Lake.

The ride

0.0 From the parking area, follow Forest Road 314 around the lake and up Daniel's Hill. The road climbs at a steep grade up to a road junction.

1.4 At the top of the hill, Forest Road 315 goes left to Lead King Basin. Make a mental note; you will be returning on this road. Continue straight on Forest Road 314 and follow it down to Lizard Lake.

1.7 Skirt the lake and climb up a short, steep hill. Drop down a steep, rocky hill and cruise along the South Fork of the Crystal River up to the Crystal Mill.

5.4 Arrive at the Crystal Mill. Hope you brought the camera. Take a break and take a few shots of the beautiful Crystal Mill.

5.7 Arrive at the small town of Crystal. The road goes straight through town, then cuts left up through a beautiful aspen forest. Climb steeply on loose tread (3) up to a road junction.

6.2 Road junction. Forest Road 314 goes straight, up to Schofield Pass. You go left on Forest Road 315 heading into Lead King Basin.

7.4 The road forks. Take the left fork and cross over a creek.

7.9 The road forks again. You stay on the main road.

8.1 Cross over the North Fork of the Crystal River. Begin climbing steeply for what seems to be miles.

9.1	Trail junction. Continue straight on Forest Road 315.
10.4	Road junction. Head left and continue on Forest Road 315.
10.7	The road splits. Stay to the left. Here comes the reward for all that climbing. Get ready for a long, fast, sometimes rocky downhill.
12.5	Road junction. Continue down on Forest Road 315.
13.9	Cross over Lost Trail Creek. Continue straight on Forest Road 315 past the Colorado Outward Bound School back to Forest Road 314.
14.7	Junction of Forest Road 314 and Forest Road 315. Go right down the fast downhill back toward Marble.
16.1	Arrive back at the Beaver Lake parking area.

Schofield Pass

Location: 28 miles south of Carbondale.

Distance: 22 miles out and back.

Time: 2.5 to 5 hours.

Tread: 22 miles on doubletrack and rough jeep roads.

Aerobic level: Moderate to strenuous with a long climb up to the top of Schofield Pass.

Technical difficulty: 2 to 4.

Hazards: A high-altitude ride with some steep hills and rough tread. Be prepared for sudden weather changes.

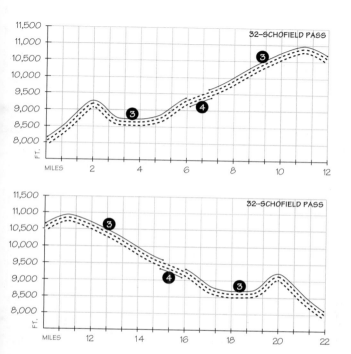

Highlights: Considered by many to be the easiest of the "pass rides" from the Aspen area to Crested Butte; features spectacular scenery, an old mining town, brilliant fall colors, and many photographic opportunities.

Land status: White River National Forest.

Maps: USGS, Pitkin County.

Access: From the intersection of Colorado 82 and Colorado 133 in Carbondale, follow Colorado 133 to the Marble turnoff. Travel 6 miles through the town of Marble to a parking area on the right at Beaver Lake.

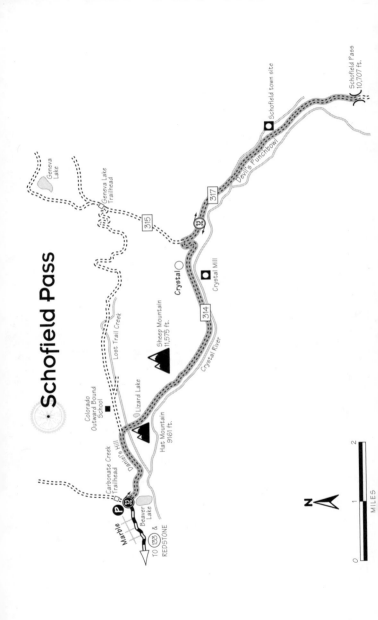

Schofield Pass

Schofield Pass
10,707 ft.

Schofield town site

Devil's Punchbowl

Schofield town site

Geneva
Lake

Geneva Lake
Trailhead

315

317

32

Crystal

Crystal Mill

Sheep Mountain
11,575 ft.

Lost Trail Creek

314

Crystal River

Colorado
Outward Bound
School

Lizard Lake

Danielle Hill

Hat Mountain
9161 ft.

Carbonate Creek
Trailhead

Marble

P

133

TO 133 &
REDSTONE

Beaver
Lake

N

0   1   2
MILES

The ride

0.0 From the parking area at the lake follow Forest Road 314 around the lake and up Daniel's Hill. The road climbs at a steep grade up to a road junction.

1.4 At the top of the hill, Forest Road 315 goes left to Lead King Basin. Continue straight on Forest Road 314 and follow it down to Lizard Lake.

1.7 Skirt the lake and climb up a short, steep hill. Drop down a steep, rocky hill and cruise along the South Fork of the Crystal River up to the Crystal Mill.

5.4 Arrive at the Crystal Mill. Hope you brought the camera. Take a break and take a few shots of the beautiful Crystal Mill.

5.7 The small town of Crystal. The road goes straight through town, then cuts left up through a beautiful aspen forest. Climb steeply on loose tread (3) up to a road junction.

6.2 Road junction. Forest Road 315 goes left into Lead King Basin. Continue straight on Forest Road 317 up a steep, loose, rocky hill (3+) into the Devil's Punchbowl. Follow the rough, steep, rocky road up to a bridge and over the Crystal River that cuts through a narrow gorge with high, rocky walls. The tread becomes quite steep and loose—no shame in pushing through this (4+) section. Crank up to a river crossing and the end of the really steep climbing.

8.0 Cross the river and go left for a nice climb to the old town site of Schofield.

8.7 Arrive at a large open meadow and Schofield. Take a break and enjoy the scenery. Follow the wide dirt road and climb at a gentle grade up to a stream crossing.

10.2	Power through the stream and make one last climb.
11.0	Schofield Pass and the top. Turn around and retrace your route back down through the town of Marble.
22.0	Back at the Beaver Lake parking area.

Glenwood Canyon Bike Path

Location: Downtown Glenwood Springs.

Distance: 30 miles out and back.

Time: 2 to 3.5 hours.

Tread: Entire ride is on a paved walking/bike path.

Aerobic level: Easy with a couple of short hills.

Technical difficulty: 1.

Hazards: This path is extremely popular with runners, walkers, and other cyclists; keep your speed in check and show courtesy to other trail users.

Highlights: A wonderful adventure for the whole family with several places to stop and enjoy the scenery; the eastern end of the path is less crowded and more peaceful.

Land status: White River National Forest and private.

Maps: USGS, Garfield County.

Access: From downtown Glenwood Springs, bike over the Grand Avenue Bridge to Sixth Street. Turn right on Sixth Street and follow to the Vapor Cave Spa and the trailhead.

Glenwood Canyon
Bike Path

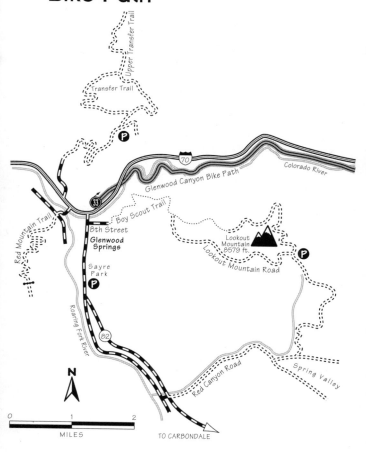

Upper Transfer Trail

Transfer Trail

🅿

70

Glenwood Canyon Bike Path

Colorado River

33

Boy Scout Trail

Red Mountain Trail

8th Street
**Glenwood
Springs**

Lookout
Mountain
8579 ft.

Lookout Mountain Road

🅿

Sayre
Park

🅿

Roaring Fork River

82

Red Canyon Road

Spring Valley

N

0   1   2

MILES

TO CARBONDALE

0.0 Follow what used to be old U.S. Highway 6 east along Interstate 70. The path crosses over I-70 on a pedestrian bridge to Horseshoe Bend and No Name.

2.0 No Name Rest Area. The path drops down to the river, then pulls away from the river on flat riding.

4.5 Grizzly Creek Rest Area. This place can be a zoo in the summer months. Slow down, or better yet walk your bike through this section.

6.0 Shoshoni Power Plant and put-in.

9.5 Hanging Lake Rest Area.

12.5 Blair Ranch Rest Area.

15.0 The end. Take a break and enjoy the scenery. Turn around and retrace your route back to Glenwood Springs.

30.0 Back at the Vapor Cave Spa. Check out the spa or take a dip in the pool at Glenwood Hot Springs.

Red Mountain

Location: Downtown Glenwood Springs.

Distance: 7.0 miles out and back.

Time: 1 to 2 hours.

Tread: 7.0 miles on dirt road.

Aerobic level: Moderate with a good climb to the top of Red Mountain.

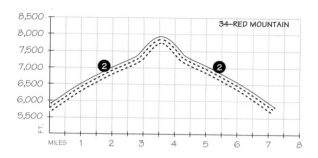

Technical difficulty: 2 to 3.

Hazards: This is a popular trail; be on the lookout for other trail users. Use caution on the fast downhill back to the trailhead.

Highlights: Awesome hill climb following an old ski-area service road; not too technical uphill, fast and fun downhill.

Land status: City of Glenwood Springs.

Maps: USGS, Garfield County.

Access: From downtown Glenwood Springs, go west on Seventh Street, which soon turns to West Eighth Street. Cross over the Roaring Fork River and turn right on Midland Avenue. Follow Midland Avenue to Red Mountain Drive. Go left on Red Mountain Drive to West Ninth Avenue and up to a parking area for the Red Mountain Trail. The mileage starts here.

The ride

0.0 Start cranking up the obvious dirt road, past a large water tank.

2.0 The grade becomes steeper as you pedal up the east

115

· Red Mountain

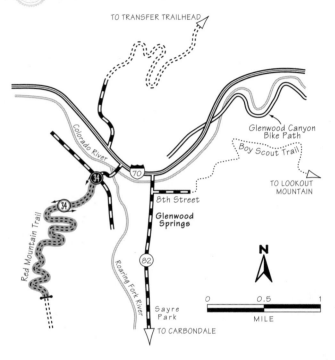

TO TRANSFER TRAILHEAD

Colorado River

Glenwood Canyon
Bike Path

Boy Scout Trail

70

34

34

TO LOOKOUT
MOUNTAIN

8th Street

Glenwood
Springs

Red Mountain Trail

N

Roaring Fork River

82

Sayre
Park

0   0.5   1

MILE

TO CARBONDALE

flank of Red Mountain. Great views up Glenwood
Canyon and Lower Roaring Fork Valley.

2.5 The grade gets even steeper.

3.5 You are now at the top of Red Mountain. Take a break
and enjoy the scenery. Private property lies ahead.
Turn around and follow the road back to the parking
area.

7.0 Back at the trailhead parking area—what a great
downhill!

35

Red Canyon Road

Location: Downtown Glenwood Springs.

Distance: 15.2 miles out and back.

Time: 1.5 to 2.5 hours.

Tread: 5.6 miles on paved roads, 9.6 miles on dirt roads.

Aerobic level: Easy with a good climb to the top of Red Canyon Road.

Technical difficulty: 1 to 2.

Hazards: Car traffic.

Highlights: An excellent workout, the route stays dry in the early spring months; access to the Boy Scout Trail and other Forest Service roads.

Land status: City of Glenwood Springs and White River National Forest.

Maps: USGS, Garfield County.

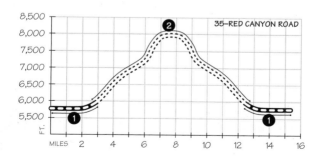

Red Canyon Road

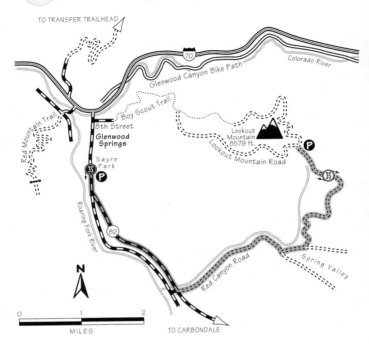

Access: From downtown Glenwood Springs, head up the valley on Grand Avenue (Colorado 82) for 1.2 miles to Sayre Park on the left. The mileage starts here.

The ride

0.0 From Sayre Park, ride up valley on Grand Avenue (Colorado 82). At the second light, go right across the railroad tracks and drop down to a stop sign.

0.6	Continue straight on South Grand Avenue, traveling along the east side of the Roaring Fork River up to the Buffalo Valley Restaurant and Colorado 82.
2.7	Cross Colorado 82 (use caution) to Red Canyon Road.
2.8	Begin a long climb up Red Canyon Road (115 Road).
5.5	Junction with 119 Road. Continue straight on 115 Road.
5.9	Turn left onto 120 Road (Lookout Mountain Road). Keep cranking uphill on this sometimes rutted, rocky road.
6.6	The road forks. Bear right.
7.6	Arrive at a large parking area and the Forest Hollow Trailhead. Stop here. Take a rest before retracing your route back to Sayre Park.
15.2	Back at Sayre Park.

Boy Scout Trail

Location: Downtown Glenwood Springs.

Distance: 19.5-mile loop.

Time: 2 to 4 hours.

Tread: 5.6 miles on paved roads, 7.6 miles on dirt roads, 6.3 miles on singletrack.

Aerobic level: Moderate with a good climb to the top of Red Canyon Road.

Technical difficulty: 1 to 3 on the doubletrack, 3 to 4 on the downhill singletrack section.

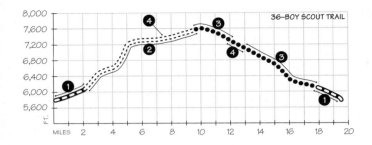

Hazards: Car and four-wheel-vehicle traffic. The downhill off of Lookout Mountain is steep and tight.

Highlights: A good long ride on a variety of surfaces, featuring a hair-raising singletrack descent with great views to the city and Glenwood Canyon.

Land status: City of Glenwood Springs and White River National Forest.

Maps: USGS, Garfield County.

Access: From downtown Glenwood Springs head up valley on Grand Avenue (Colorado 82) for 1.2 miles to Sayre Park on the left. The mileage starts here.

The ride

- **0.0** Travel up valley on Grand Avenue (Colorado 82). At the second light, go right across the railroad tracks and drop down to a stop sign.
- **0.6** Continue straight on South Grand Avenue, traveling along the east side of the Roaring Fork River up to the Buffalo Valley Restaurant and Colorado 82.
- **2.7** Cross Colorado 82 (use caution) to Red Canyon Road.

Boy Scout Trail

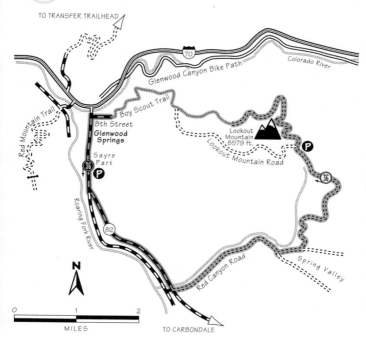

2.8   Begin a long climb up Red Canyon Road (115 Road).

5.5   Junction with 119 Road and great views up valley to Mount Sopris. Continue straight on 115 Road.

5.9   Turn left onto 120 Road (Lookout Mountain Road). Keep cranking uphill on this sometimes rutted, rocky road.

6.6   The road forks. Bear right.

7.6   Arrive at a large parking area and the Forest Hollow Trailhead. Go right on the Forest Hollow Trail.

8.0 The road forks. Continue straight up the rutted four-wheel road.

8.3 Gate and barbed wire fence. Continue straight toward the power lines.

9.2 Arrive at a fence and trail marker. Continue under the power lines and down the hill.

9.5 Trail marker. Go left onto a wide singletrack trail. Here's the payoff for all that uphill riding. Singletrack for the next 6 miles.

10.2 Arrive at an often-wet, marshy area. Take the single-track going off to the left and enjoy 2 miles of rolling singletrack.

12.2 Rocky, technical (4+) section: use caution. Arrive at a signed trail junction. Continue straight. Awesome views of Glenwood Canyon.

15.7 The trail splits. Go right and head down the steep, rocky, narrow singletrack trail. This is good stuff here.

16.4 Trail junction. The Forest Hollow Trail goes right. You go left, then make a quick right down another awesome singletrack trail. Enjoy 2 miles of tight, downhill singletrack with some steep switchbacks and rocky (3 to 4) sections.

18.3 The trail ends at a private house and driveway. Go right down to Grand Avenue, then turn left onto Grand Avenue and pedal up valley to Sayre Park.

19.5 Back at Sayre Park.

37

Boy Scout Trail Uphill

Location: Downtown Glenwood Springs.

Distance: 7.4 miles out and back.

Time: 1 to 2 hours.

Tread: 6.4 miles on singletrack and 1.0 mile on paved road.

Aerobic level: Strenuous with a steep, continuous climb up to Lookout Mountain.

Technical difficulty: There is a section of steep climbing that could be 5 if you can stay on the bike; 1 on paved roads.

Hazards: Car and four-wheel-vehicle traffic on the roads, and hikers on the singletrack: keep your downhill speed in check. The downhill off of Lookout Mountain is steep and tight.

Highlights: A challenging climb with panoramic views once atop Lookout Mountain; fun downhill back to the trailhead.

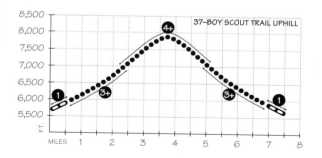

Boy Scout Trail Uphill

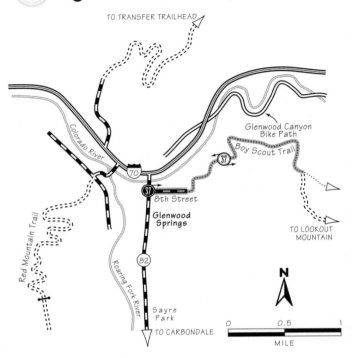

TO TRANSFER TRAILHEAD

Colorado River

Glenwood Canyon
Bike Path

Boy Scout Trail

37

70

37

8th Street

Glenwood
Springs

Red Mountain Trail

Roaring Fork River

82

TO LOOKOUT
MOUNTAIN

Sayre
Park

TO CARBONDALE

N

0   0.5   1

MILE

Land status: City of Glenwood Springs and White River National Forest.

Maps: USGS, Garfield County.

Access: The mileage starts at the intersection of Grand Avenue and Eighth Street in downtown Glenwood Springs.

The ride

0.0 Go east up Eighth Street to the start of Boy Scout Trail.

0.5 Turn left at the kiosk and crank up a short, steep, rocky section.

0.8 Cross over a small bridge.

0.9 Steep hill ahead. Crank hard and keep those legs moving.

1.4 Very steep, rocky hill climb.

1.9 Another steep (4) hill climb; views out to Glenwood Canyon.

2.3 Crank up a short, steep hill.

2.5 Abandoned old truck. The trail mellow outs for the moment.

3.0 Go left onto Forest Hollow Trail, then make a quick right up the Boy Scout Trail (5). This is the crux of the ride. Give it all you've got and then a little more.

3.7 Lookout Mountain and the top of the ride. Take a break and have a seat at one of the picnic tables. Turn around and retrace your route back to Glenwood Springs.

7.4 Back in Glenwood Springs.

Transfer Trail

Location: Downtown Glenwood Springs.

Distance: 5.3-mile loop.

Time: 1 to 2 hours.

Tread: Rough jeep road.

Aerobic level: Strenuous with a good climb to the 2-mile mark.

Technical difficulty: 3 to 5.

Hazards: Downhill section is fast, rocky, and steep. A popular four-wheel-drive road: watch for vehicles and other trail users.

Highlights: A short but intense ride, with a challenging uphill and a fast, rocky descent; stunning views.

Land status: White River National Forest.

Maps: USGS, Garfield County.

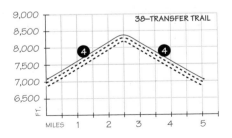

·Transfer Trail

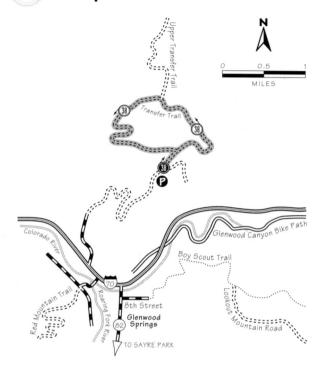

Access: Take exit 116 off Interstate 70 to Glenwood Springs. Turn left at the first traffic light onto Sixth Street (U.S. Highway 6), then turn right onto Traver Trail Road. Follow it for 0.4 mile to Transfer Trail Road on the right. Go right up the dirt Transfer Trail Road, passing a Transfer Trail sign, and travel 2 miles to a pullout/parking area overlooking an old mine site. Mileage for the ride starts just up the road at a metal sign marking the Transfer Trail.

The ride

0.0 At the sign, begin an uphill battle on a rough, four-wheel-drive road.

0.5 A road goes off to the left. Continue straight.

0.9 Another road goes off to the left. Continue straight and get ready for steep (4) climbing up a rough section. No shame in pushing here.

1.0 The road goes left and climbs steeply up to a road junction.

2.1 Road junction. Go left into and through the large open meadow. Make a quick right where the road splits.

2.3 The road forks again. Pedal right and follow the faint doubletrack to the Transfer Trail.

2.8 Go left and down. Get ready for more than 2 miles of downhill fun or terror, depending on your skill level.

3.1 A road goes off to the right. You continue straight and down.

4.8 Back at a familiar trail junction and calmer waters. Turn right.

5.3 Back at the metal sign. Hey, it's good to be back home again.

Resources

Colorado Division of Wildlife
6060 Broadway
Denver, CO 80216
(303) 297–1192

Forest Service
Aspen Ranger District
806 West Hallam
Aspen, CO 81611
(970) 925–3445

White River National Forest
900 Grand Avenue
Glenwood Springs, CO 81601
(970) 945–2521

Sopris Ranger District
620 Main Street
Carbondale, CO 81623
(970) 963–2266

Bureau of Land Management
Glenwood Springs Field Office
50529 Highways 6 & 24
Glenwood Springs, CO 81601

Rentals/Bike Shops

There are many fine bike shops in Aspen and the Roaring Fork Valley that will be more than willing to rent you a bike, sell you a bike, repair your bike, and give you information on trails and access in the area. Feel confident in calling or stopping by any of the shops listed below for your biking or outdoor needs.

Ajax Bike & Sport
635 E. Hyman Avenue
Aspen, CO 81611
(970) 925–7662
Repairs, rentals and supplies

Ajax Bike & Sport
419 Main Street
Carbondale, CO 81623
(970) 963–0128
Repairs, rentals and supplies

Ajax Bike & Sport
132 Midland Avenue
Basalt, CO 81621
Repairs, rentals and supplies

Aspen Velo Bicycles
465 Mill
Aspen, CO 81611
(970) 925–1495
Repairs, rentals and supplies

BSR Sports
210 7th Street
Glenwood Springs, CO 81601
(970) 945–7317

Life Cycles Bikes
903 Highway 133
Carbondale, CO 81623
(970) 963–2453
Repairs and supplies

Life Cycles Too!
715 Cooper Avenue
Glenwood Springs, CO 81601
(970) 945–4386
Repairs and supplies

Sunlight Mountain Bike Shop
309 9th Street
Glenwood Springs, CO 81601
(970) 945–9425
Repairs, rentals and supplies

Camping or Shelter

You can spend four or five hundred dollars a night for accommodations in the Aspen area, or spend as little as five dollars a night in one of the many fine National Forest campgrounds located throughout the Roaring Fork Valley. Call the Forest Service for information and reservations. For those of you on a strict budget, check out the campsites along Prince Creek Road in Carbondale or at the start of the Basalt Mountain rides near El Jebel. The camping is free and they are located near some fine rides.

Access

Aspen and the Roaring Fork Valley are located in the mountains of central Colorado. Interstate 70 runs east to west across the state of Colorado and Aspen and the Roaring Fork Valley can be easily accessed from exit 116 off Interstate 70 in Glenwood Springs. Aspen is blessed with a small but popular airport. Feel free to fly your Learjet into Aspen or take one of the many shuttle flights available from Denver International Airport.

Party Time

Aspen is a party town. Aspen has a very active nightlife for such a small town and you have a wide variety of choices, including bars, nightclubs, theaters, opera, and movie theaters. It also has a great selection of restaurants to choose from to fit almost any taste and budget. Just remember that the farther you travel down valley, the lower the cost for almost everything. Contact the Aspen Chamber of Commerce for more information on restaurants and lodging.

Altitude

Aspen and the Roaring Fork Valley are situated in a beautiful valley below towering, snowcapped mountains. Most of the rides in this book start at elevations of 7,000 feet or above and some rides climb up to above 12,000 feet. Those folks coming from sea level will feel the effects of high altitude riding. The symptoms for altitude sickness are headaches, fatigue, dizziness and nausea. Your body is working much harder to do a lot less than what you can do at sea level. Take your time, drink lots of fluids and don't over-extend yourself. A mile of riding at 2,000 feet above sea level is quite different than riding at 10,000 feet or higher. Short, hard sections and uphills that would be a breeze at sea level become all out grunts at higher altitudes and can zap the energy and strength from the fittest cyclists.

Weather

The average daytime temperature for Aspen in July is eighty degrees: perfect for mountain biking. But don't be fooled. In the mountains the weather changes very quickly. I have been snowed on in July on Pearl and Taylor Passes. If you're going into the mountains on what seems to be a perfect summer day, be prepared for the worst! The sudden weather changes can turn an enjoyable mountain tour into your worst mountain bike nightmare. The temperatures can drop drastically in just minutes and beautiful blue sky can turn black and ugly very quickly. Those shorts you were wearing when you started are all but useless when wet and covered with cold mud and snow. That cute sleeveless biking jersey you wear when riding in the lowlands is not going to do you much good when the summer thunderstorms hit and you are ten miles from the trailhead and your car. Be prepared!

When to Ride

Late spring to late fall is the best time to ride in Aspen and the Roaring Fork Valley. Summer months are just wonderful in the mountains and offer welcome relief from the hot temperatures in the lower lying area. The summer flowers are in full bloom by July and most of the trails are free of snow by this time. The fall is just spectacular with cooler temperatures, fewer tourists and the changing of the colorful aspen trees.

A Short Index of Rides

Glossary

ATB: All-terrain bicycle; a.k.a. mountain bike, sprocket rocket, fat tire flyer.

ATV: All-terrain vehicle; in this book ATV refers to motorbikes and three- and four-wheelers designed for off-road use.

Bail: Getting off the bike, usually in a hurry, whether or not you meant to. Often a last resort.

Bunny hop: Leaping up, while riding, and lifting both wheels off the ground to jump over an obstacle (or for sheer joy).

Clamper cramps: That burning, cramping sensation experienced in the hands during extended braking.

Clean: To ride without touching a foot (or other body part) to the ground; to ride a tough section successfully.

Clipless: A type of pedal with a binding that accepts a special cleat on the soles of bike shoes. The cleat clicks in for more control and efficient pedaling and out for safe landings (in theory).

Contour: A line on a topographic map showing a continuous elevation level over uneven ground. Also used as a verb to indicate a fairly easy or moderate grade: "The trail contours around the canyon rim before the final grunt to the top."

Dab: To put a foot or hand down (or hold on to or lean on a tree or other support) while riding. If you have to dab, then you haven't ridden that piece of trail clean.

Downfall: Trees that have fallen across the trail.

Doubletrack: A trail, jeep road, ATV route, or other track with two distinct ribbons of tread, typically with grass growing in between. No matter which side you choose, the other rut always looks smoother.

Endo: Lifting the rear wheel off the ground and riding (or abruptly not riding) on the front wheel only. Also known, at various degrees of control and finality, as a nose wheelie, going over the handlebars, and a face plant.

Fall line: The angle and direction of a slope; the line you follow when gravity is in control and you aren't.

Graded: When a gravel road is scraped level to smooth out the washboards and potholes, it has been graded. In this book, a road is listed as graded only if it is regularly maintained. Not all such roads are graded every year, however.

Granny gear: The lowest (easiest) gear, a combination of the smallest of the three chain rings on the bottom bracket spindle (where the pedals and crank arms attach to the bike's frame) and the largest cog on the rear cluster. Shift down to your granny gear for serious climbing.

Hammer: To ride hard; derived from how it feels afterward: "I'm hammered."

Hammerhead: Someone who actually enjoys feeling hammered. A type-A personality rider who goes hard and fast all the time.

Kelly hump: An abrupt mound of dirt across the road or trail. These are common on old logging roads and skidder tracks, placed there to block vehicle access. At high speeds, they become launching pads for bikes and inadvertent astronauts.

Line: The route (or trajectory) between or over obstacles or through turns. Tread or trail refers to the ground you're riding on; the line is the path you choose within the tread (and exists mostly in the eye of the beholder).

Off-the-seat: Moving your butt behind the bike seat and over the rear tire; used for control on extremely steep descents. This position increases braking power, helps prevent endos, and reduces skidding.

Portage: To carry the bike, usually up a steep hill, across unrideable obstacles, or through a stream.

Quads: Thigh muscles (short for quadriceps) or maps in the USGS topographic series (short for quadrangles). Nice quads of either kind can help get you out of trouble in the backcountry.

Ratcheting: Also known as backpedaling; pedaling backward to avoid hitting rocks or other obstacles with the pedals.

Sidehill: Where the trail crosses a slope. If the tread is narrow, keep your inside (uphill) pedal up to avoid hitting the ground. If the tread tilts downhill, you may have to use some body language to keep the bike plumb or vertical to avoid slipping out.

Singletrack: A trail, game run, or other track with only one ribbon of tread. But this is like defining an orgasm as a muscle cramp. Good singletrack is pure fun.

Spur: A side road or trail that splits off from the main route.

Surf: Riding through loose gravel or sand, when the wheels sway from side to side. Also heavy surf: frequent and difficult obstacles.

Suspension: A bike with front suspension has a shock-absorbing fork or stem. Rear suspension absorbs shock between the rear wheel and frame. A bike with both is said to be fully suspended.

Switchbacks: When a trail goes up a steep slope, it zigzags or switchbacks across the fall line to ease the gradient of the climb. Well-designed switchbacks make a turn with at least an 8-foot radius and remain fairly level within the turn itself. These are rare, however, and cyclists often struggle to ride through sharply angled, sloping switchbacks.

Track stand: Balancing on a bike in one place, without rolling forward appreciably. Cock the front wheel to one side and bring that pedal up to the one or two o'clock position. Now control your side-to-side balance by applying pressure on the pedals and brakes and changing the angle of the front wheel, as needed. It takes practice but really comes in handy at stoplights, on switchbacks, and when trying to free a foot before falling.

Tread: The riding surface, particularly regarding singletrack.

Water bar: A log, rock, or other barrier placed in the tread to divert water off the trail and prevent erosion. Peeled logs can be slippery and cause bad falls, especially when they angle sharply across the trail.

Whoop-dee-doo: A series of kelly humps used to keep vehicles off trails. Watch your speed or do the dreaded top tube tango.

Acknowledgments

Here we go. Thanks are due to a number of fine folks who somewhere along the way helped with this book. Thanks to my son Jeremy for all those wonderful days we spent together riding in the Aspen area. Our time together in these beautiful mountains is forever etched in my mind as some of the best days I have ever had. Thanks to Ed at Ajax Bike & Sport for all the help on this project and giving Jeremy his first job in a bike shop: he has turned out to be a great wrench. Thanks to all the bike shops in Aspen and the Roaring Fork Valley who support mountain biking and for answering all those questions that I was forever asking. Thanks to all the public agencies for maintaining the trails and being such a great stalwart of these great lands. Thanks to my son Adam and my daughter Rachael for all your support and help. Thanks to Nala my beautiful female Labrador, who when all my other partners bail out, was always ready to go and never complained. And last but not least to my wife Laurel, thanks for your constant support on what is just another excuse to get me into the mountains.

Bob D'Antonio
June 2001

About the Author

Bob D'Antonio lives in Louisville, Colorado, with his wife, Laurel, and his three children. He is a native of Philadelphia, Pennsylvania, and has spent many hours biking, climbing and hiking throughout the United States. Bob has been mountain biking since 1982 and has written several regional mountain biking guides for Falcon Publishing. During his 27 years of climbing, Bob has established over 600 first-ascent rock climbs and has authored three rock-climbing guides.

Bob's previous Falcon Guides include: *Rock Climbing Colorado's San Luis Valley; Classic Rock Climbs #04 Garden of the Gods/Pikes Peak, Colorado; Classic Rock Climbs #03 Mueller State Park/Elevenmile Canyon, Colorado; Mountain Biking Denver/Boulder;* and *Mountain Biking Grand Junction and Fruita.* He is currently working on other Falcon Guide titles.